READING GANDHI

READING GANDHI

DR. KUSUM LATA CHADDA

KANISHKA PUBLISHERS, DISTRIBUTORS
NEW DELHI-110 002

KANISHKA PUBLISHERS, DISTRIBUTORS
4697/5-21 A, Ansari Road, Daryaganj
New Delhi-110 002
Phones : 2327 0497, 2328 8285
Fax : 011-2328 8285
e-mail: kanishka_publishing@yahoo.co.in

Reading Gandhi

First Published 2008

ISBN 978-81-8457-084-7

PRINTED IN INDIA

Published by Madan Sachdeva for Kanishka Publishers, Distributors, 4697/5-21A, Ansari Road, Daryaganj, New Delhi-110 002, Typeset by Sunshine Graphics, Delhi, and Printed at Nice Printing Press, Delhi.

If humanity is to progress, Gandhi is inescapable. He lived, thought and acted, inspired by the vision of humanity evolving toward a world of peace and harmony. We may ignore Gandhi at our own risk.

—Dr Martin Luther King Jr.

The Prologue

The course on 'Reading Gandhi' was introduced by Delhi University in 2004. It was introduced as a Concurrent Paper for students taking up Honours courses in Humanities, Languages and Mathematics. It is also offered as a paper in lieu of modern Indian language.

'Reading Gandhi' is a popular paper and a fairly good number of students opt for it. There is no prescribed textbook for this paper; the University has given out a list of readings. These readings are fragmentary in nature and are difficult to follow especially for those students who have no background of intellectual movements related to modernism and postmodernism. On teaching this paper for a couple of years, I realized the need of a book that could help students understand the background of the prescribed readings; hence this project. It is a challenging task because the paper is innovative; it combines political theory with the study of Gandhian thought.

The syllabus is divided into four parts. My book also follows the same pattern. Part I deals with the methods of reading a text. This part familiarizes the students with different ways of reading a text. The textual and the contextual methods are discussed, followed by a detailed discussion on Quentin Skinner and Terence Ball's landmark essays dealing with the reading of texts or classics. To make it easier for students to understand this section, a chapter on modernism and postmodernism is added right in the beginning of Part-I.

Part II is about 'close reading' of Gandhi's seminal work, Hind Swaraj. *Close reading here is the textual reading of* Hind Swaraj *where the students are expected to read the book in the original without any commentary to influence their reading. In this section I have highlighted the main points discussed by Gandhi in each of the chapters of his book, emphasizing the thread of discussion that runs through the discourse.*

Part III deals with commentaries by eminent scholars on the writings or thoughts of Gandhi. In this section the commentary by A.J. Parel is an application of the various methods of reading text discussed earlier (in Part-I of the syllabus). This section also contains commentary by Bhikhu Parekh on Gandhi's 'critique of modernity'. At this point, after a textual reading of Hind Swaraj *(required in Part II) students are already familiar with what Gandhi had written about modern civilization. Thus Parekh's essay gives them a new perspective on Gandhi's views on the subject. Parel's account also deals at length with Gandhi's critique of modern civilization with emphasis on the sources of Gandhi's thoughts. Hardiman's views on 'alternative modernity' of Gandhi carries this discussion forward. Hardiman seeks to link Gandhi's views with the present times. This section also includes a discussion on 'satyagraha', the core concept of Gandhian philosophy. This is discussed with reference to the views of Bhikhu Parekh, who is known for his views regarding the practicability of some of Gandhi's concepts. The students are thus exposed to different points of view that are generally not discussed in school classrooms. My contribution in this section is to relate the different perspectives to the earlier discussion and also to clarify the original concepts as given by Gandhi.*

The last part of the syllabus deals with reform movements led by Gandhi and his views on some of the social issues. Gandhi's stand on untouchability and the ways of removing it, is part of an ongoing discussion on the issue of reservations, as is the debate on the difference in the views of Dr Ambedkar and Gandhi on the issue. Therefore, this topic adds a sense of connectivity with the present times in an important way. I have brought the discussion to the latest developments in the field, thus giving it a contemporary touch.

Another important issue which is widely disputed and discussed even today is the issue of communal unity and Gandhi's stand on it. Gandhi's views on communal unity, on the Hindu-Muslim question and his possible role in the Partition of the country – are areas the modern-day youth ought to be familiar with in an objective way. Gandhi's views on communal unity are closely connected with his idea of, what Hardiman calls, the concept of 'inclusive nation'. In the present times when the idea of nation has again become relevant

Gandhi's views provide a perspective very different from those discussed and promoted today. These topics are dealt exhaustively with reference to the latest writings on the themes.

Gandhi's views on women have evoked a variety of responses. His views on the issues of equality of women, their role in social and political affairs and their general status in society had to be discussed with great care so that Gandhi is neither misunderstood nor unnecessarily praised. I have tried my best to do so.

The nature of the topics makes it clear that the reading of Gandhi is in continuation to the movement in the West that began with the interpretation of texts of political philosophy and then moved on to the reinterpretation of the constitutional acts and laws and then to the reading and reassessment of texts that belonged to the non-Western tradition. Of late, West's interest in Gandhi has made the reinterpretation of Gandhi a natural consequence of this quest. An additional chapter on the relevance of Gandhi is added to emphasize the necessity of reading Gandhi today.

I have tried to capture the spirit behind the new course. The division of chapters is strictly according to the syllabus with extensive notes and cross references to clarify the concepts/ideas further. The language is kept simple and the main body is not cluttered with difficult themes or discussions; they are kept in footnotes for those who would like to explore further. Difficult themes are simplified and sometimes charts and diagrams are used to facilitate understanding.

Last but not least, my book is a labour of love, a gift for students from a teacher who would like them to move on in life with the right knowledge.

KUSUM LATA CHADDA
Reader, Department of Political Science,
PG DAV College,
University of Delhi

Acknowledgements

This being my maiden venture at book writing, I needed lots of support from my family, friends and colleagues, which I received in full measure. My family encouraged me at every step of writing and gave me all the logistic support I needed. My friend and colleague Dr. Sunder Raman, Reader, Department of Political Science, PGDAV College, Delhi, read the whole manuscript with patience and gave valuable suggestions to improve the text. Another senior colleague Sh. Sushil Gupta, helped me clarify my views on the theoretical aspects of interpretation through discussions and patient hearing. Ms Seema Das, Reader, Department of Political Science, Hindu College, Delhi, was kind enough to lend me books from her personal collection.

I am also thankful to my students who through discussions and questions helped me articulate my ideas with more clarity. My son, Pranav, who also happens to be a student, prevented me from getting pedantic by insisting on simple language and expressions. In spite of all this 'cooperation' I am sure there is room for improvement. Constructive criticisms, comments and suggestions from readers are welcome.

Lastly, I would also like to place on record the help given to me by the staff of Nehru Museum Library and Indian Institute of Public Administration Library.

KUSUM LATA CHADDA

Contents

PART–IV

CONCEPTS AND MOVEMENTS

PART–I
WAYS OF READING A TEXT

I know
You believe you understand
What you think I said but,
I am not sure you
realize that what you heard is not
What I meant.

— Robert McClosky

1
The Background: Modernism and Postmodernism

Postmodernism is incredulity towards metanarratives.
–Jean-Francois Lyotard

At the core of the syllabus of 'Reading Gandhi' is the book *Hind Swaraj* which is well-known for its criticism of modern civilization, variously described by scholars on Gandhi as 'critique of modernity'[1] or the Gandhian concept of 'alternative modernity'[2] or as indicative of 'postmodern Gandhi.'[3] In the light of these discussions it is important that students know something about the concepts of modernity/modernism and Postmodernity/postmodernism. Hence, a brief discussion on these two themes follows.

Modernism, as understood by western scholars,[4] is associated with the developments in science and technology that occurred in the West in the later part of the 17th century that had consequences for the social order, the political order and the general way of thinking of the people later in the late eighteenth and early nineteenth century. Enlightenment and Industrial Revolution are considered to be two important triggers of modernity. The features of modernity that largely resulted from these two developments were dynamism, and, belief in progress and power of human reason. Modernism is believed to have originated in USA rather than Europe.[5] Modernity questioned all conventional ways of doing things. It sought to substitute the authority of God with the authority of science, economic growth, democracy or law.

Industrialization brought in its wake technological inventions including the invention of motor-cars and railways. All these developments brought about a change in the thinking of individuals who started valuing punctuality, specialization, uniformity and standardization. The need for specialization led to further division of labour. While Karl Marx called this division antagonistic, Emile Durkheim, another sociologist, believed that this could at some stage lead to organic unity. In the process of division of labour not only work but home, leisure, religion were all split up.[6] Assembly-line production was also done by these new industries where components of larger machines were produced in bulk and assembled later. Since Henry Ford was the pioneer in this field, assembly line mass production came to be called 'Fordism'.[7]

Thus while Karl Marx gave us the concept of commodity, and Durkheim the world of detailed subdivisions based on tasks and responsibility, another sociologist, Max Weber gave us the concept of rationalization reflected in scientists' work in the laboratories, or in the businessman's ledgers or in bureaucracy. This idea of machine-like precision became the hallmark of much of art, literature and architecture of modernity as well.

A byproduct of rationalization was the growth of city or urban lifestyle. This lifestyle was also reflected in the attitudes of city-dwellers, marked by aloofness, formal and contractual relations. The architecture was impacted where men like Le Corbusier conceptualized cities from the vantage point of car drivers leaving no room for pedestrians.[8]

The idea of rationalization and discipline led to the valorization of control. The orderliness in city reflected this control. The idea of hierarchy and control was reflected in the structure of military as well. Homogeneity and control were in evidence in the concept of nation state. Control was the operating principle in factories. Household table manners reflected control. The description by Foucault of the Panoptican prison plan[9] was the epitome of modern discipline, in which the prisoners, unsure of being watched by prison authorities, maintained internal surveillance and discipline. In this way a new form of control replaced the omnipresent God of the medieval ages.

Modernity had its downside too. Karl Marx wrote about the exploitation of workers by capitalists and the feeling of alienation among workers. Durkheim found that the division of labour led to a feeling of restlessness among human beings that was almost suicidal in nature. He suggested that some normative basis of society was needed. Weber hinted that too much of rationalization was crushing the human spirit.[10]

In the 1960s there was a feeling that a new kind of society was emerging. This sense was captured by sociologist Daniel Bell who in his book *The Coming of the Post-industrial Society(1973)* put down the thesis that the factory worker image of the industrialism has now been replaced by the new professional and technical elite of the service sector, helped by new information and communication technology. Though this phenomenon was considered to be continuation of modernity, some believed that it had some strains of postmodernism that was to come shortly. Building on Bell's idea of post industrial society, Lyotard wrote his essay 'The Postmodern Condition' (1979) in which he painted the picture of a world beyond progress. The theme of progress which was so central to modernisation was thus abandoned.

Postmodernism is generally believed to be a movement of ideas arising from, but also critical of elements of modernism. Because of the wide range of uses of the term, some elements of modernity are chosen as being continuous while other elements of modernity are critiqued.

The argument of the postmodernists is that economic and technological conditions of our age have given rise to a decentralized, media-dominated society. The media creates images of things around us which are copies of each other. Same is the case with ideas which have no real, original, stable or objective source for communication and meaning.

Globalization, brought on by innovations in communication, manufacturing and transportation, is often cited as one force which has driven the decentralized modern life, creating a culturally pluralistic and interconnected global society lacking any single dominant centre of political power, communication, or intellectual production. The postmodern view is that inter-subjective knowledge and not objective knowledge is the dominant form of discourse under such conditions and the ubiquity of copies and dissemination, fundamentally alters the relationship between reader and what is read, between observer and the observed, between those who consume and those who produce.

One strand of postmodernism, known as 'poststructuralism' tends to see all knowledge—history, anthropology, literature, psychology etc as *textual*. This means that *knowledge is not just composed of concepts but also of words.*, e.g., the dictionary meaning of 'cow' may not explain much or anything definite to a person who has not seen the animal. Poststructuralism is a movement associated with a wave of thinkers such as Jacques Derrida, Julia Kristeva, Roland Barthes, Gilles Deleuze, Felixe Guattari and Michel Foucault.

Another strand of postmodernism has been the idea of 'deconstruction' which is borrowed from the German philosopher Martin Heidegger's concept of *Destruktion* meaning the study of 'ultimate rock bottom reality'.

As a result of these two movements the idea of a fixed meaning of text is dropped. The text is open to a free play of meanings. Deconstruction is thus a tactics of decentering, a way of reading which first makes us aware of the centrality of the term. Then it attempts to *subvert* the central term so that the marginalized term temporarily overthrows the hierarchy. For example the diagram given below can be read in two ways: one, by describing it as a diagram depicting two human faces facing each other; other, depicting a candle. Until eyes are added to the opposite human faces or wick is added to the candle, the diagram can be interpreted either way.

Diagram-1[11]

Deconstruction first focuses on the binary oppositions within a text—like man/woman. Next it shows how these opposites are related, how is that one of these is central, natural and privileged, and the other ignored, repressed and marginalized (a good example of this could be subaltern themes in history). Next, it temporarily undoes or subverts the hierarchy to make the text mean the opposite of what it originally appeared to mean. Then in the last step both terms of opposition are seen dancing in a free play of non-hierarchical, non-stable meanings. In the diagram given below the figure can be read as a big triangle composed of many small triangles. What is the number of these triangles? Which triangle is within or outside which one? All these questions can not be answered in a definite way. They can be answered in a variety of ways. Which triangle is the central or the most important triangle is difficult to say. Which of the triangles are peripheral or less important is also difficult to point out. Hence there is a play of meanings in the reading of the diagram, giving rise to a floating meaning.

Diagram-2[12]

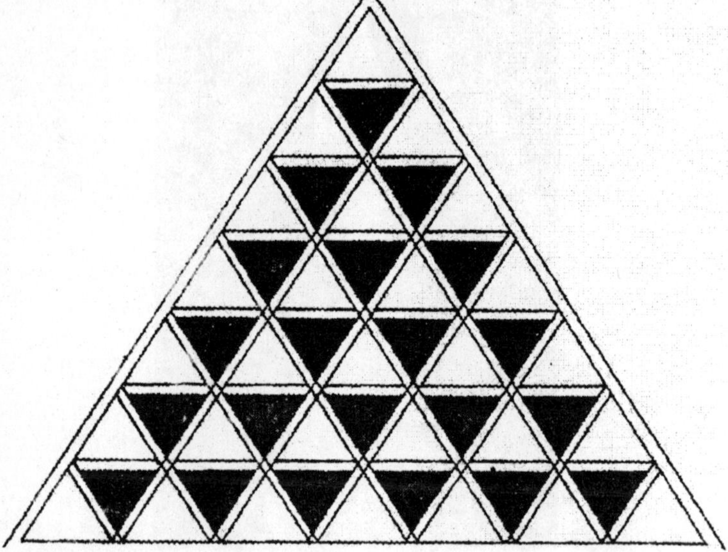

According to Derrida textuality is realizing 'how' a text means rather than 'what' a text means. It is a realization that a text is made up of 'words' and words can mean different things.

There is a debate on whether postmodernism is a positive or a negative movement even among people who use this term.

Chart-I

Ihab Hassan, a postmodern theorist compares modenism and postmodernism in the following way[1]

Modernism	*Postmodernism*
Form	Antiform
Purpose	Play
Design	Chance
Hierarchy	Anarchy
Art object/finished work	process/performance

(Contd.)

Modernism	*Postmodernism*
Presence	Absence
Centering	Dispersal
Genre/Boundary	Text/intertext
Root/depth	Rhizome/surface

Briefly this means that while modernism emphasized a set form, postmodernism is totally against any such finality of form. Modernism explores the purpose behind a text or phenomena, for postmodernists, there is floating purpose where at one time one purpose becomes important at another time another purpose. Modernism believes in structures of a particular design, postmodernism leaves things to chance. Hierarchy of power, or relations, is present in modernism but absent in postmodernism. Modernism aims at finalization while postmodernism is a process, a performance, and, therefore, never final. Modernism looks for the presence of something whereas postmodernism laments the absence of something. Discovery of centre is the aim of modernism, while postmodernism enjoys dispersal. The modernists fit a text into some genre or give it a boundary, whereas the text in postmodernism is intertextual and therefore its meaning keeps on changing. Finally, the allegory of modernism is a plant rooted in one place while postmodernism resembles a rhizome with roots along or under the ground with roots and stems growing from it.

REFERENCES

1. Bhikhu Parekh,*Gandhi,* OUP, 1997.
2. David Hardiman, *Gandhi in his times and ours,* Permanent Black, 2003.
3. Lloyd I. Rudolph and Susanne Hoeber Rudolph, *Postmodern Gandhi and other essays,* OUP, 2006.
4. There is an alternative view of modernism as well. Hardiman has alluded to it while discussing Gandhi defining his views as indicative of 'alternative modernity'.
5. David Lyon, *Postmodernity,* Vivagraoup Pvt. Ltd, New Delhi, 2002, p. 26.
6. *Ibid.,* p. 30.
7. *Ibid.,* pp. 26-27.

8. *Ibid.*, p. 32.
9. The idea was the invention of the late nineteenth century political thinker, Jeremy Bentham.
10. Lyon, *op.cit.*, pp. 35-41.
11. Taken from Jim Powell, *Derrida for Beginners,* Orient Longman Ltd, India, Delhi, 2000, p. 24.
12. *Ibid.*, p. 29. Powell describes it thus: If you have a system of triangles such as this, then you will notice that if you stare at it , a series of configurations of triangles present itself to your vision—one after another. But each so called *present* configuration, each group of triangles which seem to be momentarily *present,* had emerged out of a *prior* configuration and is already dissolving into a *future* cnfiguration.
13. Jim Powell, *Postmodernism for Beginners,* Orient Longman Ltd, Delhi, 1998, p. 17.

2
Ways of Reading a Text: Textual and Contextual

There are a lots of things I don't understand – But from 50 years in this game., I have learned two things (1) I can ask friends who work in these areas to explain it to me at a level that I can understand, and they can do so, without particular difficulty; (2) if I am interested I can proceed to learn more so that I will come to understand it. Now Derrida, Lacan, Lyotard, Kristeva, etc – even Foucalt, whom I knew and liked, and who was somewhat different from the rest – that I also don't understand, but (1) and (2) don't hold: no one who says they do understand can explain it to me and I haven't a clue as to how to proceed to overcome my failures. That leaves me one of the two possibilities: (a) some new advance in intellectual life has been made: perhaps some sudden genetic mutation, which has created a form of "theory" that is beyond quantum theory, topology, etc., in depth and profundity; or (b) ...I wont spell it out.

–Noam Chomsky

Meaning of 'Text'

According to the *Oxford Advanced Learners Dictionary*, as a noun, 'text' means 'the main printed part of a book or magazine, not the notes, pictures etc'; or "any form of written material', or 'the written form of a speech, a play, an article'. Thus any written word, sentence, paragraph, story, novel or any book either written with hand, by a computer, or printed, as different from 'spoken', may be considered a text. Text is different from the spoken word and covers a wide range of written expressions.

However, some postmodernists of the deconstruction strain define text broadly as to encompass not just written words, but the entire spectrum of symbols and phenomena.

There are many ways of reading a text, the two most popular being the textual and the contextual.

THE TEXTUAL METHOD

The textual method believes that the reader needs only to read the text over and over again in order to understand its meaning. The writer in his/her wisdom makes an all out effort to convey to the reader whatever he/she wishes to convey and there is therefore no need to know even who the writer of the text is, when and under what social and political circumstances he/she wrote. It is also irrelevant to even try to discover what the author intended to write unless the author himself states his intention. The supporters of this view believe that once the book is in public domain the author is dead or is irrelevant. It now depends on the readers to interpret and understand the meaning of the text. It is therefore, perfectly valid for the same text to be interpreted in different ways in different periods of time or by different readers.

There are generally three ways in which the textual method is interpreted:[1]

(a) According to objectivists the meaning of the text 'is contained' in the text, and must be 'extracted' by the reader. Such a model of communication is 'transmissive' which in other words means that *meaning of a text can be transmitted from the 'sender' to the passive 'receiver'*.[2]

(b) The second type of textual reading is 'constructivist'. According to this a *text is an interplay between writers and readers*. In other words, this means that a text cannot speak for itself: it needs a reader as well as a writer.

(c) The third is the 'subjectivist' interpretation which believes that *meaning is entirely in its interpretation by readers*, that it is 'recreated'.

Derrida and the Deconstructionist View

To this method of reading text, an important contribution was made by Derrida, the famous deconstructionist. Derrida argued that a text is merely 'a collection of words'. The meaning of the text becomes intelligible if it is deconstructed in terms of gender, class, religion, country and so on of the author as well as the interpreter The best way to read a text is to consider it as a play of meanings, where sometimes the central becomes peripheral and sometimes the peripheral becomes central or *vice versa*.. An example of the central and the peripheral mode of reading is the 'subaltern school' of history in India with which most of the students are familiar, where for the first time, the role of tribals and other ignored sections in the freedom struggle of India was recognized. Earlier, history writing focussed mainly on the happenings in the north of India and that too about the doings of kings and emperors. The common people were completely ignored in so far as their contribution was concerned.

The author is dead

In literature the textual approach is reflected in the theme of the 'author is dead' declaration. The idea of the author's *disappearance* has a long history in the century.

According to a contemporary tradition of interpretation, the author is radically disengaged from the interpretive process, that 'the book divides the act of writing and the act of reading into two sides, between which there is no communication' (Paul Ricoeur, 'What Is a Text?'). This tradition is a main support of one of the most influential of the Reader-Response theories. As Ricoeur, commenting on the fact that writing separates the writer from the reader, remarked, 'Sometimes I like to say that to read a book is to consider its author as already dead and the book as posthumous.'

In his best-known work, the essay 'The Death of the Author' (1968) Roland Barthes saw the notion of the author, or authorial authority, in the criticism of literary text as suggestive of an ultimate meaning of the text. He argued that by imagining an ultimate intended meaning of a piece of literature one could infer an ultimate explanation for it. But the fact of the matter is that the variety of meaning in language and the unknowable state of the author's mind makes any such ultimate realization impossible. Therefore the whole notion of the 'knowable text' is a delusion created by the Western bourgeois culture because the idea of giving a book or poem an ultimate end means that one treats it as consumable, something that can be used up and replaced in a capitalist market.

Barthes goes on to differentiate between what he calls the *writerly text*, in which the reader is active in a creative process, and a *readerly text* in which he/she is restricted to just reading.

Readerly Text: A text that makes no requirement of the reader to 'write' or 'produce' his or her own meanings. The reader may passively locate 'ready-made' meaning.[3].

Writerly Text: is a text that aspires to the proper goal of literature and criticism: '... to make the reader no longer a consumer but a producer of the text'. Writerly texts and ways of reading constitute, in short, an active rather than passive way of interacting with a culture and its texts. 'A culture and its texts', Barthes writes, 'should never be accepted in their given forms and traditions. As opposed to the 'readerly texts' as 'product', the 'writerly' text is ourselves writing, before the infinite play of the world is traversed, intersected, stopped, plasticized by some singular system (Ideology, Genus, Criticism) which reduces the plurality of entrances, the opening of networks, the infinity of languages.' Thus reading becomes for Barthes 'not a parasitical act, the reactive complement of a writing,' but rather a 'form of work'.

Textual Interpretation in Law

Somewhat similar meaning of the word textual is found in the legal terminology as well. *Textualism* is a formalist theory of statutory interpretation which holds that a statute's ordinary meaning should govern its interpretation, as opposed to inquiries into non-textual sources such as the intention of the legislature in passing the law, the problem it was intended to remedy, or substantive questions of the justice and rectitude of the law. It should not be confused with the "plain meaning" approach, a simpler theory first used prominently in the early Burger Court in cases such as Tennessee Valley Authority v. Hill [4] which looked to the dictionary definitions of words, without reference to common public understanding or context.

CONTEXTUAL METHOD

Contextual reading of a text means reading a text keeping in view the social and historical environment in which it was written. It attempts to understand a philosophical position in terms of its relation to the intellectual movementsof its day and those earlier philosophies that may have influenced its development.

According to M J Osler contextual studies could be of two types:

(*a*) one focussing upon the context of other philosophical ideas surrounding a philosophical argument and,
(*b*) focussing upon the social and historical context within which a philosopher developed his arguments.[5]

The supporters of contextual approach argue that a historically oriented course offers a much better stimulus to critical thinking than 'contemporary problems' oriented approach. Another supporter of the approach has suggested that compared to a properly historial introduction to philosophy, a problem based course built around a series of contemporay articles is 'professionally self-aggrandising, pedagogically unwise philosophically unproductive'.[6] Contextual approach, the supporters believe contributes, therefore, to the development of critical philosophical attitude.

On the practical side, some believe that contextual approach leads to the development of transferable skills. The practitioners of this approach are familiar with methods of research; have the competence to manage large and diverse quantities of information; develop the capability to accumulate, select and interpret a wide range of material, the ability to organise information in a logical and coherent manner which is very important for the understanding and analysis of issues, events and people.[7]

REFERENCES

1. The following discussion borrows inputs from Daniel Chandler's essay 'Text and Construction of Meaning' which is adapted from his book *The Act of Writing at http://www.aber.ac.uk/media/Documents/short/texts.html*
2. Views of D.R. Olson, 'From Utterance to Text: The Bias of Language in Speech and Writing' in Daniel Chandler(ed) *The Act of Writing*, Online book, 1995.
3. Roland Barthes,*S/Z: An Essay*, ISBN 0-374-52139-5, p. 200.
4. US Supreme Court, 1978.
5. M. J. Osler, 'The *History* of Philosophy and the History of *Philosophy*: A Plea for Textual History in Context', *Journal of History and Philosophy*,40/4, 2002, pp. 529-33.
6. J. J. McDermott, 'The Teaching of Philosophy— Historically', in T Kasachkoff (ed), *In the Socratic Tradition: Essays on Teaching Philosophy*, Lanham: Rowman and Littlefield, 1998, p. 179.
7. Appleton, *Your Degree in History: What Next?* AGCAS, Signpost Sheet, 2001.

3
Quentin Skinner: 'Meaning and Understanding in the History of Ideas'

Quentin Skinner's treatment of political theory as a dimension of political life marks a revolutionary move in the historical as well as philosophical study of political thought. Skinner brings the study of political theory closer to the language of agents and treats theorists as politicians of a special kind.

—Kari Palonen, *Quentin Skinner: History, Politics, Rhetoric.*

Quentin Skinner, Regius Professor of Modern History at Cambridge University, along with co-historians John Dunn and J.G.A Pocock, (together known as the founders of the 'Cambridge School') is credited with paying attention to the 'languages' of political thought. In order to understand political thought, these historians hold, one needs to be familiar with its particular 'language' which constitutes 'idioms, rhetorics, specialised vocabularies and grammars' considered as 'a single though multiplex community of discourse.' It is the job of historians to uncover or discover them in texts and later, 'learn' them so as to be able to interpret how political thought can be stated in historically discovered 'linguistic universes'.

Quentin Skinner as important representative of the Cambridge School published a landmark essay 'Meaning and Understanding in the History of Ideas' in 1969. This essay created a stir in intellectual circles as Skinner pointed out the inadequacy of the available methods, both the textual and the contextual, of reading text, and described the earlier interpretations of political thinkers as *mythologies of history,* underlining their unscientific nature.

As against the earlier methods, Skinner gave his own new *contextual and more historically sensitive a*pproach to reading a text that aimed at recovering the *author's intention i*n order to understand what she/he was writing. His method applied the recently popularized, *speech- act theory*[1] according to which the author's intention could be truly deciphered if one examined what the author was *doing* while writing something. In this way one could know the *meaning* of the text. The next step was to know the *intended force* with which the author *did* something. This, according to Skinner, would help in *understanding* the text. Thus, Skinner believes that the *linguistic strategy* employed by an author is a significant tool for discovering the intentions of the writer with regard to a text.

Quentin Skinner applied his approach in his study of the works of important political thinkers. To understand his approach better a look into how he applied it to the study of Machiavelli's famous work *The Prince* could be of help. Machiavelli's advice to the 'Prince' that 'Princes must learn when not to be virtuous'[2] is examined by Skinner. On the face of it this is a simple statement, and yet it has been the source of much debate. Trying to discover the meaning of this piece of advice is not easy, and Skinner has argued that the original Italian word that is often translated as 'virtuous' - *virtú* - is impossible to render directly into English, representing a complex of different attributes, and that it should be left in its original form so as to avoid any form of misinterpretation. In the case of Machiavelli's text, the intention of the author could be deciphered and correctly interpreted by situating the author in the particular *historical and philosophical context* in which he wrote. That is how the discovery of the *intended force* of the statement of a writer can be made. The text has to be situated in a biographical, social, political and literary context rich enough to enable an inference to be drawn about the intended meaning of it. Skinner argues that in the case of Machiavelli this necessitates the study of all texts containing advice to rulers written in the time when he was writing. For this purpose other texts of the times, both minor and major, are surveyed to identify the ideology, and also, the points of departure. In other words, Skinner's approach studies 'text in context'. In addition it also makes it clear that great texts do not generally conform to the ideology of their times. They are different from their times and are for this reason treated as classics.

Quentin Skinner's Criticism of Current Approaches/'Mythologies'

Usually political thought has been discussed in two ways: one, as a *procession of writers* whereby the political thoughts of writers who are considered to be important are given generally, in a chronological order e.g., as the political thought of Plato, Aristotle, Machiavelli Hobbes, Locke, Rousseau, Bentham, JS Mill, Marx and so on. The other method of explaining political thought is the *unit idea* method which seeks to categorize authors in terms of ideas they were supposed to enunciate and thus discusses various authors under the headings of ideas like liberty, equality, justice, political obligation, and feminism and so on. In both the approaches the *method* that is followed for determining what ideas should be associated with which writers is either *textual reading of their writings* (i.e., reading the text under the assumption that the reading itself would clarify the meaning as an independent work that stands on its own), or of *giving the context undue importance* without reference to the intention of the writer.

Skinner objects to all such approaches and states that in these approaches *history is treated as a myth* because they do not follow a scientific method or the right method to arrive at conclusions. Since the method is faulty the conclusions arrived at are also flawed.

THE MYTHOLOGY OF DOCTRINES

The first 'myth' Skinner seeks to demolish is the *mythology of doctrines* [3] which is the belief that 'each classic writer (in the history, say, of moral or political theory) will be found to enunciate some doctrine on each of the topics regarded as constitutive of the subject.' This myth sometimes takes the form of "converting some scattered or incidental remarks by a classic theorist into their 'doctrine' on one of the expected themes". Skinner cites the case of associating the fourteenth century thinker Marsilius with the theory of 'Separation of powers', a theory, which according to Skinner, took shape many centuries after his death. He expresses surprise that even those who deny the possibility of Marsilius being associated with the doctrine do soon the basis of his text and not on the 'impropriety of supposing that he *could* have meant to contribute to a debate the terms of which were unavailable to him.'[4]

Another danger that follows from this myth is that 'of too readily finding expected doctrines in classic texts'. Thus Locke is associated with the idea of government based on consent whereas what he was doing in his theory of trusteeship, according to Quentin, was appealing to one of the familiar legal analogies in the political writings of the period. Skinner wonders if 'the writer meant to articulate the doctrine with which they are being credited, why is it that they so signally failed to do so, so that the historian is left reconstructing their alleged intentions from guesses and hints?'[5]

Skinner also examines the *mythology of doctrines vis-a -vis* the *unit idea* approach developed by Arthur Oncken Lovejoy, the professor of Philosophy at John Hopkins University. According to Lovejoy history of ideas should focus on 'unit ideas', i.e., single concepts generally given a one word name, and study how unit ideas combine and recombine with each other over time. Quentin argues that this approach leads to the *hardening of an idea* and the *mistaken belief that the idea in question had existence in history* and thinkers either failed to notice it, or could not come to the level of noticing it or that it simply 'dropped from sight' at various times. The unit idea approach also may lead to the 'absurdity' of 'anticipations' of a doctrine in earlier writers who are congratulated for being 'clairvoyant', for example, a writer who may not have even thought of a particular idea is sometimes given credit of being the one of the earliest supporters of the idea which came many centuries later. Further, argues Quentin, one encounters 'a connected absurdity in the endless debates whether a given 'unit idea' may be said to have 'really emerged' at a given time whether it is 'really there' in some given writer'. He elaborates this absurdity by referring to the theory of separation of powers. Though the idea of separation of powers emerged with the writings by Montesquieu in the eighteenth century some philosophers of the sixteenth century are congratulated for anticipating it in their writings!

The second error the mythology of doctrines vis-à-vis the unit idea approach is that it may assume that a classic theorist who fails to come up with a recognizable doctrine on one of the mandatory themes has fallen short of his proper task or goal. Thus Plato's *Republic* is criticized for omitting the influence of public opinion, the concept that was unknown during his lifetime. Another flaw of the mythology of doctrines is that after arbitrarily assigning a particular idea to a writer, he is criticized for *not being consistent*.

THE MYTHOLOGY OF COHERENCE

The second great myth Skinner refers to is the expectation of coherence in the works of great authors. Thus in search of coherence statements of intentions by writers are *discounted if they do not fit into the general idea,* or sometimes even whole works are *discounted if they seem to impair general system of thought*. Skinner cites the example of how Hobbes' stated intention is ignored and he is declared guilty of being incoherent with regard to something that he never intended to write about. Similarly, 'Marx is not allowed to have developed and changed this mind from the humanistic strains of the *Economic-Philosophical Manuscripts* to the apparently more mechanistic system outlined over twenty years later in volume I of *Das Capital'*.[6] (The former refers to the manuscripts discovered in the twentieth century wherein Karl Marx talks about his theory of alienation whereas the latter is a critique of capitalism which is the basis of his theory of class war and revolution. Most of the writers associate Marx with only the latter theory ignoring his humanistic leanings). Skinner criticizes historians who seek to justify the so-called lack of coherence in writings by stating that maybe the writers were *deliberately being incoherent so as to escape persecution.* These historians commit the error of doing so without substantiating their claims with facts.

Skinner is of the opinion that the two mythologies referred above are because of the fact that while assessing a writer's work the *historians of ideas have some presumptions about the discipline to which the writer is supposed to have contributed.* For example, Hobbes' thought is supposed to belong to the discipline of political science and therefore, his works are examined from the point of view of how a political theorist would write. This leads one to think that perhaps when a work is examined as an independent work this problem may not arise. Skinner believes that this may not be so. He writes that even in such cases, when 'considering what significance some particular text may be said to have for us, it is rather easy in the first place to describe the work and its alleged relevance in such a way that no place is left for the analysis of what its author may have intended or meant.'[7]

THE MYTHOLOGY OF PROLEPSIS

Presumption of the above nature, according to Skinner, leads to a type of discussion that might be labeled as the *mythology of prolepsis.*[8] This mythology is in evidence in the characterization of Plato and Rousseau as supporters of totalitarianism. 'In both cases an account that might be true of the historical significance of the work" is put along with an 'account of what the author was doing' and thus creating an entirely new thing. The historical significance of the work is how these authors were used by rulers to justify their actions but it does not mean that either Plato or Rousseau were supporters of totalitarianism i.e., a non-democratic government.

Another flaw in earlier writings, according to Quentin Skinner is that at times the *author is described as being one with his theory*. Locke, for instance, is considered to be the founder of liberal political thought and also characterized as a 'liberal' person, which may not be true.

PAROCHIALISM

Other dangers that lurk for a historian of ideas may take two particular forms of *parochialism.* An argument in one work may happen to remind the historian of a similar argument in another or an earlier work. Or a later work may appear to contradict an argument found in an earlier work. In either case the historian may mistakenly come to suppose that it was the intention of the later writer to refer to the earlier, and so may come to speak misleadingly of the 'influence' of the earlier work. Though there may be cases of genuine influences, but Skinner cautions historian against the temptation to fall in the trap of unverified influences. He advises that such verification can be possible if *(a)* B is known to have studied A's work *(b)* that B could not have found the relevant doctrines in any writer other than A; and *(c)* that B could not have arrived at the relevant doctrines independently.

The second form of parochialism could be that historians may misuse their vantage point in describing the *sense* of a given work. They may form a view about the age in which the writer would be writing and fit him in the general mood of the times, a fact which may not be true in case of at least some of the writers or some of the movements. Quentin Skinner gives the example of the Leveller Movement in England of the seventeenth century, which, among other things, asked for rights. Describing the Levellers as liberals according to the 'sense' of the times is problematic because they were staunch supporters of monarchy.

Lastly, Quentin Skinner points out that even when one zeroes in one's analysis to the thinking process of a writer one should tread warily. Thinking itself is a complex process and a writer may not always present his thoughts coherently. Therefore, looking for coherence or even collecting scattered thoughts of writers and putting them together amounts to tampering with their ideas.

Toward the end of his essay Quentin arrives at two 'positive conclusions'. According to him, 'The first concerns the appropriate method to adopt in studying the history of ideas. The understanding of texts, I have suggested, presupposes the grasp of what they were intended to mean and of how that meaning was intended to be taken.... After this, the next step must be to trace the relations between the given utterance and this wider linguistic context as a means of decoding the intentions of the given writer'. About the second general conclusion he says that it 'concerns the value of studying history of ideas. The most exciting possibility here is that of a dialogue between philosophical analysis and historical evidence.'[9]

Skinner modifies his earlier stand in 2002 when he recognizes the importance of history of ideas and a possibility of a dialogue between philosophical analysis and historical evidence. He concludes the 2002 version of his essay with the statement 'to demand from the history of thought a solution to our own immediate problems is to commit not merely a methodological fallacy but something like a moral error. But to learn from the past—and we cannot otherwise learn at all—the distinction between what is necessary and what is contingently the product of our own local arrangements is to learn one of the keys to self -awareness itself.'

Critical Appreciation of Quentin Skinner's Approach

Critics argue that Quentin Skinner's approach cannot be successfully applied to all social sciences. Kenneth Minogue, for instance, argues that historians take into consideration the historical situations whereas a political idea may stand on its own. Hence Skinner's approach may not be good enough for the study of political thought.

Terence Ball in his article, which is discussed in the following chapter, also criticizes Skinner for giving writers' intention undue importance. He argues that while it is important to know what the writer intended in writing a particular text, the text has a life of its own and the consequence of a text may be very different from, or even the opposite of, what the writer may have intended. A study based on the 'reception' of a text, its interpretation and reinterpretation is the right method of reading a text. A text should also be examined from the point of view of interest of the interpreter, Ball argues.

Quentin Skinner's approach was hailed as an approach that was bound to have many positive consequences. Apart from contributing a new approach to the study of social sciences and history, his approach underlined the necessity of studying lesser-known political writers as a means of shedding light on the classic authors. Skinner has also challenged the assumption that political classics are monolithic and freestanding. His ideas have been a major influence in interpretation of texts throughout the world, not only philosophical or historical texts but also laws and acts. The merit of Skinner's approach lies in the fact that as expressed by James Tully 'Skinner is not solely concerned with history and method, but also with using both to throw light on the present.'[10]

How is Quentin Skinner's Approach Relevant to Reading Gandhi

Quentin Skinner emphasizes the study of the intention of the author in understanding a text. In the discussion that follows it would become evident how valid this argument is in case of Gandhi's writings, especially his seminal work *Hind Swaraj*. Gandhi states that his intention in writing the book was to tell the revolutionaries in India that they could not gain independence from British rule through violence. When we probe further and examine the books that Gandhi lists as his readings in the appendix of *Hind Swaraj* we discover that Gandhi's intentions in writing the book were far deeper than what he stated them to be. He was in fact attacking modern civilization which he held responsible for many ills affecting both the English and the educated Indians. This becomes evident after one studies *Hind Swaraj* inter-textually, i.e., with reference to the writings available to Gandhi during the writing of *Hind Swaraj* and the writings he actually read and imbibed.[11] Critiques of modern civilization had been attempted by writers like John Ruskin, Leo Tolstoy, Carpenter and many others, described today as the 'other West' and Gandhi was influenced by them. This approach looks similar to the one applied by Skinner with reference to Machiavelli in order to understand why Machiavelli advised the Prince to ignore virtues sometimes, a view contrary to the accepted morals of the times. Gandhi criticized modern civilization at a time when most of the educated Indians, including his trusted lieutenants like Jawaharlal Nehru and Sardar Patel were under its spell. Gandhi's choice of marching on a road less taken can be explained thus.

REFERENCES

1. The 'speech act' is a concept in linguistics and philosophy of language. Before the advent of this theory language was viewed as a way of making factual statements. The other uses of language were not acknowledged. JL Austin and later his student, John Searle developed a theory which we now know as the speech act theory. According to this theory when a person says something he is in fact doing something. For example when one says 'good morning' one is *greeting*, when one says 'sorry' one is *apologizing* or if one says 'could you move a bit' one is actually *requesting* or *ordering*.
2. Machiavelli was a 16th century Italian political philosopher who is famous for his book *The Prince*. In this book Machiavelli gives a series of advice to the ruler with regard to effective administration.
3. Quentin Skinner, "Meaning and Understanding in the History of Ideas" in Quentin Skinner (ed), *Visions of Politics*, Vol. I, CUP, Cambridge, 2002, p. 59.
4. *Ibid.*, p. 60.
5. *Ibid.*, p. 61.
6. *Ibid.*, p. 71.
7. *Ibid.*, p. 72.
8. Prolepsis is a figure of speech in which a future event is referred to in anticipation e.g., a character who is about to die might be described as a 'dead man'. It is also referred to in anticipation of an objection. As a philosophical concept it was used in ancient epistemology to indicate a so-called 'preconception', i.e a pre-theoretical notion which can lead to true knowledge of the world.

9. Quentin Skinner, "Meaning and understanding in the history of ideas' in *Visions of Politics :Regarding Method,* Cambridge University Press, 2002, pp. 86-87.
10. James Tully, 'The Pen is a Mighty Sword: Quentin Skinner's Analysis of Politics', in James Tully, (ed) *Meaning and Context: Quentin Skinner and his Critics,* Polity Press, UK, 1988.
11. This is discussed at length in Chapter V.

4
Terence Ball on How to Read a Classic[1]

A classic is a book that has never finished saying what it has to say.

—Italo Calvino

Terence Ball in his book *Reappraising Political Theory: Revisionist Studies in the History of Political Thought* (Clarendon Press, Oxford, 1995) has put forward his views on how to read a classic. In the preface of the book Ball justifies the need for such an exercise because he believes that the 'study of political thought requires the reinterpretation and reappraisal of—to use a now- contentious term—the 'classics' of political theory' (Preface, viii).

Need for Reinterpretation

In the introductory chapter of the book with the title, 'How to read a classic', Ball starts with the question that is normally asked from a historian of ideas as to why political classics are read again and again and also reinterpreted several times. Are they difficult to understand by dimwitted people? Or do political scientists keep on reinterpreting them just to increase their number of publications in order to secure their jobs? These questions are not only asked by people who are outside academia but also from sections within the academia. The *behavioralists*, in the discipline of Political Science, for instance, complained about the futility of the study of long dead thinkers and asked political scientists to focus on scientific theories of political behaviour. People from the discipline of *analytic philosophy* who could be expected to be sympathetic to the study of classics, want political scientists to focus on economic, rational choice and game theoretic models, and theories regarding the concerns of liberty, justice etc., rather than interpret old classics. The other section that objects to the study of classics constitutes the *proponents of multiculturism.* This group celebrates the empowerment of the marginalized sections and therefore has serious objections to the study of classics which, they believe, would promote the thinking of elite, chauvinistic males, i.e., 'dead white men' at the expense of the importance of women, blacks, gays and other minorities.

Against these objectors are pitted the supporters of the reading of classics. At the head of this group was Leo Strauss who took up cudgels against behavioralists[2] and then made a case for the reading of classics for which he earned the epithet—'neo-conservative'.

Terence Ball claims that both the positions i.e., of the objectors and the supporters are extreme positions. On the one hand, he does not approve of making a fetish of methods, as was done by the objectors, and in the process making method an end in itself, on the other, he also does not share the enthusiasm for classics as shown by Leo Strauss and his followers

Terence Ball believes that *reappraising classics is a necessity that no political scientist can afford to ignore.* This is amply proved by the fact that the need for reinterpretation is not of recent origin. It had been there even before writing had originated. At that time totems and dreams were interpreted. Later songs that represented oral tradition were interpreted from different points of views. Aritstotle's *Poetics,* written about 2500 years ago, is also a treatise on how to read a classic and is followed by students even today.

At the same time there have been parallel movements that exhorted scholars to 'get back to basics'. This movement asked writers to stick to the text and not interpret it. It also advocated trying to recover the author's intention in writing the text and then reading the text accordingly. In both the cases the call was to give up interpretation altogether. The supporters of this line of thought have been in law and literature and also among religious leaders. These scholars are of the opinion that layers and layers of interpretation hide the original text and in the process distort it. The example of the famous Protestant Martin Luther is the most apt from the field of religion. In law some judges in USA call for a return to the 'original intent' of the constitution makers[3]. In the field of literature scholars like Susan Sontag are the main supporters of the idea that classics should not be interpreted.[4]

INESCAPABILITY OF INTERPRETATION

Terence Ball argues that whether we like it or not, we cannot escape interpretation. He writes: 'The decision to interpret or not to interpret is not an option open to human beings, but a requirement that comes, so to speak, with the territory of being human. For our language-using and meaning-seeking species, interpretation is inescapable.'[5] It is connected with our nature of existence. The fact of the matter is that we do not come across raw or virgin data in our lives because the words we come across are already invested with meaning. In addition, as individuals we have our own baggage of historical and cultural predispositions from which vantage point we make sense of the world around us. These two views, the world's and ours, achieve a fusion in our lives (which Gadamer calls the 'fusion of horizons'). In this manner we create our own interpretation which may be an improvement upon or is simply different from what we received from the world.

Interpretation is not a luxury but a necessity. As communicating and interacting social agents we have to interpret the actions, utterances and practices of other people. Sometimes it could also be a matter of life and death, as in case of interpretation of law by the courts/lawmaking or enforcing authorities.

INTEREST OF THE INTERPRETER

When we are aware of the context in which we are interpreting it is easy to come to a correct interpretation of an action, behaviour or utterance. The difficulty, however, arises in an alien culture with which we are not familiar. This situation is analogous to the situation in which a historian of political thought finds himself while reading something produced in a culture different from his own, both in terms of time and space. In such a clueless circumstance it is the 'interest' of the writer in a particular text that determines the meaning of the text. This 'interest' is not simply the interest in the author but it is deeper interest that provides the ground for, and possibility of, interpretation—a standpoint from which an enquiry can begin and interpretation proceed.

The 'interests' of the reader could be varied. It could be *contemporary* interest in a text e.g. what can a particular author teach us on liberty today. The 'interest' could be *historical* such as why a particular author wrote the way he did on liberty. The interest could also be in the nature of an enquiry into the *main targets* of that particular text or its *intended audience*. The interpretation could also be with reference to the *literary style* used by the author and what was the effect of this on the readers. The interpreters could also be looking for *antinomies* or *oppositions* in a particular work. Similarly the interests could also be *logical or philosophical* in nature such as looking for coherence and consistencies or examining how well the author has presented his case. All these examples show that *the method employed by a person to read a classic is dictated by the problem at hand and the interest that interpreter seeks to serve.* For example, if a interpreter is looking at a book from philosophical perspective he may not be interested in why the author wrote the way he did as would a person whose interests are historical would do. In this sense all reinterpretation becomes value laden. It is, in simple words, interpretation of an interpretation given earlier and thus can be called a 'reinterpretation' or reappraisal.

This, however, does not mean that political scientists as members of the same discipline are in agreement over method of reappraisal. Here too we have a range of viewpoints not similar to each other. These are the neo-Marxists, the realists, the poststructuralists, deconstructionists, the Straussians, and the 'new historians' —to name a few. All these different schools of thought employ their own strategies for interpreting a text. However the most controversial, according to Ball, has been the idea of the importance of author's intentions in reading a text. Some jurists and Cambridge new historians, notably Quentin Skinner, have publicized this idea in recent years.

Terence Ball agrees with other critics of Skinner's approach and states that the recovery of 'authorial intention' is not essential, even if possible in principle. A book may lead to unintended consequences far beyond what the writer may have intended or much different from what the writer may have intended. Here Terence Ball concedes that it would be wrong to assume that intentions are totally irrelevant. *In order to know that the consequences of the texts were not the same as intended by the author one needs to know what the author intended in the first place. But the process of interpretation should not stop at the knowledge of the author's intention.* It should move along the so called 'reception' or 'reader response' theories. In other words one should bear in mind that a text is not merely an artifact produced by the author, but also a communication received by the reader. Thus, while one should be aware of the role of an author's intention in writing a text, one should also bear in mind that once a book is published it has life of its own.

Another point worth noting is that every text passes through the filter of readers which means that one should, in order to know a text fully, must also periodically reappraise the value or validity of the interpretations inherited from other writers. Terence Ball, calls this 'a three cornered fight for meaning'. It goes something like this:

> ...one interpretation of 'the data' is challenged by another, and both are assayed according to the available evidence(textual, linguistic, historical, etc). But, since such evidence is rarely, if ever, self-evident, it requires interpretation to tease out its meaning and significance for and bearing on the problem at hand. And for this

purpose a rival interpretation is indispensable. The second, or rival account, proceeds not only by reference to these data, but by way of a critique of the first's interpretation of it. This critique is into a distraction or an unfortunate necessity, but is instead an essential feature of the history of political thought.[6]

POLITICAL THEORY AS A PROBLEM–SOLVING AVTIVITY

According to Terence Ball the historical study of political theory is basically a problem-solving activity. It takes other reinterpretations as alternative solutions to some puzzle or problem and then goes on to assess their adequacy vis-à-vis each other and in relation to one' s own proposed solution. Interpretation is indeed a three cornered fight in which we take others' interpretations into account reappraising their adequacy and value. This is the crux of Ball's approach.

In the preface to the book, Ball has summarized his approach in the following words. He writes: 'My approach in the present study can be characterized in two words: *pluralist* and *problem driven*. That is, no one method of interpretation will suffice in all cases; which of many methods one chooses depends on particular problem being addressed, and not the other way round.'[7]

Towards the end of his article Ball reiterates the important features of his approach to the study of classics and invites his readers to read his work and assess the worth of his approach. These features are as follows:

- Follow a *problem centric perspective* which means that the method of interpretation varies with and is dictated by the particular interpretive problem being addressed.
- The interpretive problems can come from any source – historical, contemporary, literary, political or whatever. These problems provide interest or vantage point from which interpretation proceeds. These problems could arise from within the text or from questions raised and interpretations advanced and

defended, by subsequent commentators often in idioms that were unavailable to the author.

- It is worth trying in so far as possible and where appropriate, to *place the text within two contexts,* first being the *context of its composition* (which necessarily includes some reference to its author' s intentions), and the second being the various *contexts or its reception* (which may or may not take account of authorial intent).
- Wherever possible, show how an earlier theorist, and/ or a subsequent interpretation, casts light on contemporary problems.

Ball has used this methodology in his book *Reappraising Political Theory* and has examined the conventional view of Machiavelli as a genuinely modern theorist, Hobbes a proto-positivist, Rousseau as a totalitarian, and similarly reinterpreted the ideas believed to be held by J.S. Mill, August Comte, Bentham , Karl Marx and more recent thinkers like John Rawls, Gerald O'Neill and Richard Rorty.

To sum up, one can say that Terence Ball's approach to the study of classics seems to be an eclectic approach where the strategies for interpretation are chosen in accordance with problem in hand and also there is no hesitation in employing different strategies simultaneously.

How is Terence Ball Relevant to Reading Gandhi

While Quentin Skinner's approach emphasizes the importance of the author's intention in linguistic context in understanding a text, Terence Ball, while acknowledging the indispensability of knowing the author's intention, moves further. Once the book is in public domain it acquires a life of its own hence the context of its reception, Ball holds, acquires significance. With reference to *Hind Swaraj,* one is aware that the book had been received differently at different points of time. Anthony J. Parel has ably discussed this (in the following chapter).[8] Its present popularity is due to the hope of seeking answers for the present day problems in what it says. The popularity of

Gandhian thought in the world today is also because after exhausting all means of solving the problems of violence, war, discrimination, corruption, insensitivity, environmental degradation, and so on, the world has found in it solutions that seem simplistic, but are in fact very effective.

REFERENCES

1. Earlier the Greek writings alone were called classics. Gradually the term classic came to be associated with anything which was not contemporary and was in a class by itself i.e. no other work could reach the level of excellence it had reached. The features of a classic are supposed to be its universal appeal— across space and time— and its aesthetic value. Because of these qualities a classic always holds the attention of its admirers who tend to see a new meaning in it every time they read or see it. Interest in a classic never seems to wane.
2. Taking a dig at the 'behaviouralists' insistence on science and quantification Strauss pointed out that in the process they missed out on what was happening around them. His famous quote in this context was: 'Only a great fool would call the new political science diabolic: it has no attributes peculiar to fallen angels. It is not even Machiavellian, for Machiavelli's teaching was graceful, subtle, and colorful. Nor is it Neronian. Nevertheless one may say of it that it fiddles while Rome burns. It is excused by two facts: it does not know that it fiddles, and it does not know that Rome burns.', *Liberalism Ancient and Modern*, p. 223.
3. In the context of United States with Antonin Scalia, Clarence Thomas and Robert Bork but some liberals, such as Justice Hugo Black and Akhil Amar have also subscribed to the theory. Originalism is a family of theories, that includes *original intent*, a theory that is of the view that interpretation of a written constitution is (or should be) consistent with what was meant by those who drafted and ratified it. It is often used as justification for allowing the government to deny civil liberties to unpopular groups, such as blacks in the 1950s and gays who wish to marry in modern times on the ground that the 'founders' did not intend for blacks or gays to enjoy the same rights as white males. Another theory, the *original meaning* theory, is closely related to textualism, is of the view that interpretation of a written constitution should be based on what the ordinary meaning of the text would have been at the time it was adopted; that is, what it would have been understood to mean by reasonable persons living at the time of its ratification.
4. Susan Sontag is an important intellectual voice in America. Known as an essayist, novelist, filmmaker and activist, she is famous for her

support to literary freedom of Salman Rushdie when he was threatened with death by Iranian *fatwa.* She is also known for criticism of US policies in West Asia and refused to describe the 2001 suicide bombers as 'cowards'. In her book *Against Interpretation and Other Essays* published in 1966, in the title essay 'Against Interpretation', she argued that the emphasis which had come to be placed on the intellect under modern social and cultural conditions had given way to a new critical approach to aesthetics that was increasingly usurping the spiritual importance of art. Rather than recognizing great creative works as possible sources of energy and defense against the brute rationality and empiricism that seemed to be seeping into every aspect of western life at the middle of the twentieth century, contemporary critics were all too often taking art's transcendental power for granted, and focusing instead on their own intellectually constructed abstractions like "form" and 'content.' In effect, she wrote, interpretation had become 'the intellect's revenge upon art.' The essay famously finished with the words, 'in place of a hermeneutics we need an erotics of art'.

5. *Op.cit.,* p. 7.
6. *Op.cit.,* pp. 26-27.
7. *Ibid.,* pp. viii-ix.
8. See Chapter-VI.

PART–II

CLOSE READING OF *HIND SWARAJ*

Let my friend [referring to V.D. Savarkar and colleagues] remember that Hind Swaraj ... *as the booklet itself states, was written in answer to the revolutionary's arguments and methods. It was an attempt to offer the revolutionary something infinitely superior to what he had, retaining the whole of the spirit of self-sacrifice and bravery that was to be found in the revolutionary.*

—M.K. Gandhi

5
Close Reading of *Hind Swaraj*

I have been asked to talk on the relevance of Hind Swaraj *today. I have no solid arguments to prove the relevance of* Hind Swaraj *in today's world. Because, the relevance or irrelevance of anything depends on our attitude, our priorities and goals and there is nothing that is relevant universally. But looking at all of humanity, and in this context,* Hind Swaraj *is very relevant. It is very relevant to know how to save this earth from complete self destruction, and how to teach this humanity to live in harmony with everything around.*

—Prof. Samdhong Rinpoche, Prime Minister, Tibetan Government in Exile

(The following account is a summary of the book Hind Swaraj or the Indian Home Rule *written by Mahatma Gandhi and translated from Gujarati by him. I have used the reprint of the book published by Navajivan Press, Ahmedabad in 2005. The students are advised to read the text in full. The summary is no substitute for the original text).*

Hind Swaraj or Indian Home Rule was written by Gandhi in 1909 while he was travelling back to South Africa from England where he had gone as the head of the delegation representing the case of Indians settled in South Africa before the British Parliament. In England, he came to know about the murder of a British officer, Curzon Wyllie by an Indian youth Madan Lal Dhingra to avenge the insult to Indians at the hands of British officials in India. Gandhi was disturbed by this act of violence in the name of nationalism and was perturbed by the fact that the act had the support of majority of the youth in India. He met with some of the leaders of the groups who were not averse to gaining independence for India by killing the British. He held long discussions with them but failed to convince most of them.[1]

On his return journey, he, therefore, mulled over the whole situation and wrote the small booklet *Hind Swaraj* in an inspired state of mind. The pace at which the book was written, the absence of corrections and overwriting, later reported, shows how single- minded was Gandhi in his mission. The book was completed within ten days and was originally written in Gujarati, his mother tongue.

The book is in the form of an imaginary dialogue between an 'editor' and a 'reader'. The 'editor' represents Gandhi's views whereas the 'reader' represents the views of the 'misguided' youth of India. Gandhi moves very cautiously from one chapter to the next, dealing with the misgivings of the young and attempting to allay their doubts.

The book is divided into twenty chapters with headings of chapters not conveying much about their contents. Gandhi takes up the issue of the dissatisfaction of the youth towards the moderate leadership of the Congress party in India. He asks them to be grateful to the Moderates for the role they had played in educating the Indians on political affairs and sowing the seeds of nationalism in them. He, however, agrees that the movement against the Partition of Bengal (1905) has shown that mere petitioning is not enough and petitions need to be backed by force, which has to be moral force. He makes it clear that violence was not the proper means to achieve the goal of Indian independence and those who propagated it were under the spell of 'modern civilization'. If they gained independence by force, that would amount to replacing the British with Indians of the same mentality. Gandhi is very critical of the British institutions of Parliament, the Press and the overall system of governance. However, his criticism is confined to the institutions of the British government, not the

British people as such. The people are not to be blamed because they are also the victims of the same modern civilization. Gandhi then goes on to elaborate the features of modern civilization. According to Gandhi emphasis on bodily comforts at the expense of spiritual growth, mad consumerism, insensitivity to fellow human beings and mad rush to go ahead of others are some of the disturbing features of modern civilization which is marked by ill health, death and degradation of both men and women. Modern civilization is held in place by agents like the lawyers, doctors, modern system of medicine, use of railways and faster means of transport. Because of being under the spell of such civilization Indians have forgotten about their own superior civilization and allowed themselves to be ruled by the British. Only when Indians accept their own civilization they can achieve *swaraj,* which is a multi-layered concept for Gandhi. It stands for independence from British rule. It stands for democratic governance, in which all classes and communities have equal opportunities and power. It includes economic self-sufficiency and above all, includes, individual self-control exercised by the people of the country.

The following is a chapter-wise summary of *Hind Swaraj:*

Gandhi acknowledges the contribution of Moderates but emphasizes the need for new approach: the use of soul force

In the first Chapter, 'Congress and its Officials', Gandhi takes up the issue of widespread disillusionment of the youth with regard to the efficacy of methods adopted by the moderate leadership of the Congress party. These leaders were considered by the young people as either allies of the British rulers in India or totally ineffective. Gandhi argues that it is ungrateful on the part of the youth to forget the contributions made by the early leaders in rousing the consciousness of Indians, creating enthusiasm about the idea of nationality and giving them political education.

This imaginary discussion is in the context of the upsurge of nationalism in India exemplified by the *swadeshi* movement launched against the Partition of Bengal in 1905. No wonder the youth were disillusioned with the approach of 'petitioning' the British employed by the Moderate leadership of the Congress.

In Chapter II entitled—'The Partition of Bengal', Gandhi agrees with the 'reader' that the movement in Bengal had led to real awakening of India but hints at the contribution made by Moderates through the statement that 'the seed is never seen'. Gandhi makes a far-reaching observation in this chapter which sums up his philosophy behind the movements he launched later. He states: 'After the Partition, people saw that petition must be backed by force, and that they must be capable of suffering.' Petitioning backed by the moral force of suffering hereafter became the hallmark of all the movements launched by Gandhi. Gandhi, however, rues the fact that the Partition also brought about rift between the 'Moderates' and the 'Extremists' which was not good for the movement

Chapter III—entitled 'Discontent and Unrest', is a continuation of the discussions on the less positive aspects of the Partition. There is a slight reversal of roles between the 'reader' and the 'editor' because in this chapter it is the 'reader' who asks Gandhi as to what is his take on the unrest and discontent generated by the Partition. Gandhi replies 'This discontent is a very useful thing. As long as a man is contented with his present lot, so long it is difficult to persuade him to come out of it.'[2] Here Gandhi seems to echo JS Mill's views that it is 'better to be a Socrates dissatisfied than a fool/pig satisfied'. About unrest he simply compares it with a man stretching himself after getting up in the morning before he becomes fully alert.

Swaraj Does not Mean Indiscriminate Imitation of British Institutions

Chapter IV: 'What is Swaraj' appears contrived as it does not follow the natural sequence of discussion and all of a sudden the 'reader' asks Gandhi to elaborate upon his (the editor's) concept of *swaraj*, which the 'reader' suspects, is different from his (the reader's) view of *swaraj*. Here the deliberate use of the word *swaraj* even in the English version is significant. Gandhi does not give a clear answer to this question but proceeds to examine situations that 'do not' constitute *swaraj*.[3] Gandhi states that Swaraj for him did not stand for replacing British rule with the rule by Indians and adopting the form of government or institutions of the British.

In Chapter V : 'The Condition of England', the 'reader' picks up the thread of the definition of *swaraj* given towards the end of the last chapter and asks Gandhi to clarify why he thinks that the government of England is not worth copying for Indians. In the discussion that follows Gandhi comes down heavily on two of the most cherished English institutions - the British Parliament and the British Press. With rather uncharacteristic harshness he likens the British Parliament to a 'sterile woman and a prostitute'. Gandhi holds Parliament to be like a 'sterile woman' because in his opinion, members of the Parliament driven by their own selfish interests, create a situation where whatever is accomplished on one day is destroyed on the other. Therefore, the Parliament fails to produce anything worthwhile like a sterile woman. Parliament was also like a prostitute, because it pandered to the wishes of the party in power rather than sticking to principles for the benefit of all. Even the office of the Prime Ministers does not escape Gandhi's scathing criticism. Gandhi is convinced that even the Prime Ministers are not honest because they indulge in bribing others by offering them influential posts. Next in the line of attack is the much flaunted free British Press. The press in Britain is not principled, he opines. It keeps on changing its stand frequently thereby misleading people who tend to follow it blindly.

The only virtue found in the English people, according to Gandhi, is love for their country and uncompromising patriotism. Apart from this virtue there is nothing worthwhile in England worth copying. With regard to the rest of the features of the British culture Gandhi holds, 'If India copies England, it is my firm conviction that she will be ruined'.

In normal course of affairs this would have put an end to the argument on the question of the character of the British but since Gandhi is the writer behind the question that the 'reader' is supposed to ask, he considers it fit not to malign a people like that. So the 'reader' is made to ask the question as to the reason behind the bad state of affairs in England. Now Gandhi has the final say. He avers, 'It is not due to any peculiar fault of the English people, but the condition is due to modern civilization. It is a civilization only in name. Under it the nations of Europe are becoming degraded and ruined day by day.'

Modern Civilization

In Chapter VI entitled 'Civilization', Gandhi proceeds to define civilization but before doing so he informs the reader that he is not alone or original in his criticism of civilization but the reader is unaware of such views because 'We rarely find people arguing against themselves. Those who are intoxicated by modern civilization are not likely to write against it.'[4] Civilization has come to be defined in terms of bodily comforts it provides. Its manifestation are machines, printing presses, means of faster transport and communication facilities, sophisticated weaponry and the resultant miserable lives led by men and women, in, for example, cramped and unhygienic factories. This civilization also underrates morality and religion and is therefore totally irreligious.

Gandhi is however hopeful that soon this civilization would meet its nemesis and come to an end. 'Civilization is not an incurable disease, but it should never be forgotten that the English people are at present afflicted by it', which, in other words, means that the Indians should keep themselves away from being infected by it.

If the modern civilization has nothing to commend itself and since the English are afflicted by it, how come such sick people could not only conquer India but also continue to hold it? This is the logical question that comes to the mind of the 'reader' who seeks an answer from the learned 'editor' in chapter VII entitled 'Why India Lost?' Gandhi's considered reply is 'The English have not taken India; we have given it to them',[5] a statement borrowed verbatim from Tolstoy's *Letter to a Hindoo* that Gandhi had translated very recently. Indians could not resist the temptation of British money and their merchandise and thus helped them establish their empire in India. They continue to remain in India because of the same reason, believes Gandhi. 'We further make their job easy by quarrelling amongst ourselves', he adds.

Gandhi is perceptive enough to identify the real motive of the British conquest of India, i.e., economic greed, and the reason behind their continued existence. (Later in history, he would attack this very basis by propagating boycott of British goods and supporting the *swadeshi* movement)

(a) *Irreligious*

In Chapter VIII entitled 'The Condition of India' Gandhi reverts to the discussion on the evil effects of modern civilization and continues to discuss the same till chapter XII. Modern civilization has made India irreligious. Religion here is not taken in terms of any denomination. Gandhi holds that the modern civilization's belief that one should be engaged in worldly pursuits otherwise one would be considered lazy is irreligious because the different religions in India preach to limit our worldly desires and emphasise that only our 'religious ambitions should be illimitable'.[6] Modern civilization is also irreligious because it legitimizes the killing of innocent animals for the advancement of scientific knowledge.

(b) *Spellbinding*

The dangerous fact about the evil effects of modern civilization is that we are not even aware that it is harming us. 'Civilization is like a mouse gnawing while it is soothing us.'[7] The 'reader' at this point tries to justify the British rule for eliminating *thugs* like Bhils and Pindaris who used to loot and kill people at random. To this Gandhi responds prophetically. He argues that the British by granting us peace have turned us into a nation of cowards and have thus emasculated us. What he concludes later in the chapter has significance for the present as well. He says, 'Moreover, I must remind you who desire Home Rule, that, after all, the Bhils, the Pindaris and the Thugs are our countrymen. To conquer them is your or my work. So long as we fear our own brethren, we are unfit to reach the goal.'[8] This could very well apply to the insurgents in North East, militant groups in Jammu and Kashmir and the Naxalites.

(c) *Railways spread disease, immorality and are responsible for rural poverty*

Continuing with his discussion on the condition of India brought about by the modern civilization in chapter IX entitled 'The Condition of India (continued) : Railways', Gandhi castigates the railways in India. According to him the railways have been responsible for the continuance of British rule in India and their effective control over India. Earlier, diseases like plague would be confined to one region alone. Railways have assisted their rapid spread. Railways have encouraged people to sell their grains at far off places for higher prices thereby leading to famines in villages. Before the advent of railways, people used to take arduous pilgrimages out of the holy motives. Now journeys are comfortable therefore all sorts of people throng at holy cities thereby making them unclean.

At this point the 'reader' comes up with an argument in support of railways that had been current during those times. He asks Gandhi as to what has he to say about the undoubted contribution of railways in spreading nationalism in India? Gandhi replies, 'The English have taught us that we were not one nation before and that it will require centuries before we become one nation. This is without foundation. We were one nation before they came to India. One thought inspires us. Our mode of life was the same. It was because we were one nation that they were able to establish one kingdom. Subsequently they divided us.'[9] As proof of his statement he points out at the existence of four *mathas* (spiritual seats) in four directions of our country.[10]

(d) *Communal distrust by encouraging the idea of different nations*

The author of the book now brings the discussion between the 'reader' and the 'editor' to the most troubling questions of the time. The 'reader' accepts the argument that even before the advent of the British, India was one nation. But he is not sure whether what was true of pre- Muslim India would be true of the India of today where Mohammedans, Parsis and Christians also live in the country?

Gandhi considers the issue of Hindus and Muslims to be important enough to devote a full chapter to it. In chapter X entitled 'The Condition of India (continued): The Hindus and the Mahomedans', after a detailed discussion on the communal question Gandhi sums up: 'In no part of the world are one nationality and one religion synonymous terms, nor has it ever been so in India".[11] On the sensitive issue of cow slaughter, Gandhi does not mince words. 'If I were overfull of pity for the cow, I should sacrifice my life to save her but not take my brother's. This, I hold, is the law of our religion.'[12] Rubbishing the argument that the British have created the rift between the two communities, Gandhi states, 'If two brothers want to live in peace is it possible for a third party to separate them?' [13] Emphasizing the importance of strengthening of relations Gandhi gives the simile of an unbaked mud pot. 'The way to save the pot is not to keep it away from danger point but to bake it so that no stone would break it.'[14] Gandhi is of the firm belief that the existing mutual distrust between the two communities could be dissolved by creating mutual confidence, or 'heart-unity'.

(f) *Lawyers aggravate communal tensions, help the continuance of British rule in India*

In Chapter XI, continuing with the discussion on the condition of India, Gandhi discusses how lawyers have a ruinous effect on the civilization of our country. Though, a lawyer himself, in the role of the 'editor' Gandhi is unsparing in his criticism of lawyers. Since lawyers thrive on disputes they have prolonged feuds between Hindus and Muslims thus embittering the relations between the two communities. The 'editor' is of the 'firm opinion' that lawyers have enslaved India. He elaborates upon this in his later discussion.

Through law courts the British have tightened their hold on India because they employ Indian lawyers who help them rule the country. Had there been no Indian lawyer or judge the British rule could not have perpetuated itself, according to Gandhi.

(g) *Doctors responsible for the entrenching of British rule, breeding immorality, playing with religious sentiments of the people*

In Chapter XII Gandhi discusses how doctors have ruined India. He alludes to the historical references where the English were able to win over the faith of the local rulers by curing their relatives and thus were able to establish their hold on India. At philosophical plane, he states that hospitals have taught people not to take care of their bodies hence contributed to the making of immoral men because it was Gandhi's belief that man can never fall sick if he has control over his senses. As discussed earlier, Gandhi is also against the killing or torturing of animals in the name of experimentation. Medicines also violate our religious instinct, states Gandhi, because all sorts of animal parts or alcohol are used in the preparation of medicines. Besides medicines are priced higher than their actual cost, which amounts to cheating the public.

True Civilization is Indian Civilization

After pointing out at the evils of modern civilization, Gandhi proceeds to describe his view of civilization in chapter XIII, appropriately entitled 'What is true civilization?' He equates true civilization to Indian civilization. 'The civilization India has evolved is not to be beaten in the world.'[15] His definition of true civilization is: 'Civilization is that mode of conduct which points out to man the path of duty. Performance of duty and observance of morality are convertible terms. To observe morality is to attain mastery over our mind and our passions. So doing, we know ourselves'[16] When the 'reader' points out that how can he sing the glory of Indian civilization when the same is criticized for treating women badly, is responsible for child marriages, widowhood and forced prostitution and where the religion justifies the killing of innocent animals in huge numbers? Gandhi dismisses the arguments of the reader by saying that the instances that have been enumerated are 'defects' and cannot be equated with the ancient Indian civilization. Further he elaborates upon the crucial difference between the Indian and the modern civilization. He clarifies that while the Indian civilization attached great importance to moral elevation, the western civilization is concerned more with physical comfort and is therefore immoral.

India Can Achieve Swaraj by following Indian Civilization

Gandhi had seemingly moved away from the main topic of discussion with which he had started in the first chapter and a couple of chapters following it which was how India can win *swaraj.* In Chapter XIV Gandhi returns to the theme of Indian independence once again. To the question as to how can India become free Gandhi states that he has already answered the question indirectly and would attempt to answer it directly now. But instead of stating things very clearly Gandhi hints that *swaraj* could be attained if Indians follow the great Indian civilization and keep away from the damaging impact of the modern civilization. In that case, believes Gandhi, if the English become Indianized it would not be necessary for them to go.

(a) Violence is not a feature of Indian civilization: Italy's example not to be followed

The reader is not impressed. He argues that it was not possible for the British to change their nature, (the point Gandhi refutes) and India could gain independence from the British rule only through the use of arms as the Italians had done in the previous century. He also pointedly asks Gandhi as to what was his view with regard to Italian freedom fighters like Mazzini and Garibaldi.

Continuing the discussion on the freedom movement in Italy, Gandhi clearly opines that while Mazzini cared for the common man, others fighting for freedom were fighting only for their king. Thus Gandhi brings out a very important aspect of *swaraj* that is 'democratic government' in which the common men and women, farmers and workers, also have a say. 'My patriotism does not teach me that I allow people to be crushed under the heel of Indian princes if only the English retire.'[17] The other difference between Italy and India according to Gandhi is that Italians had arms and Indians do not possess them[18] therefore the Indians cannot fight like Italians against the British army which is well armed. At this point, Gandhi also lets out his innermost desire when he says 'the fact is that the Indian nation will not adopt arms, and *it is well that it does not.*'(italics mine) [19]

(b) Importance of ends and means in Indian civilization

So far the discussion on use of arms has been only in philosophical or indirect terms. The 'reader' now lays bare his strategy before Gandhi. He states, 'At first, we shall assassinate a few Englishmen and strike terror; and then, a few men who will have been armed will fight openly. We may have to lose a quarter of a million men, more or less, but we shall regain our land...' [20] Gandhi's response to this violent strategy is predictable. He comes down heavily on the 'reader'. He makes it known to the 'reader' that 'those who are intoxicated by the wretched modern civilization think these things. Those who will rise to power by murder will certainly not make the nation happy. Those who believe that India has gained by Dhingra's act and other similar acts in India make a serious mistake. Dhingra was a patriot, but his love was blind. He gave his body in a wrong way; its ultimate result can only be mischievous.'

The 'reader' persists and points out that sometimes such acts frighten the government into giving concessions as was done in the Morley-Minto reforms of 1909.Gandhi on his part is convinced that whatever, if any thing, is given out of fear would remain as long as that fear lasts.

This argument brings the discussion between the 'reader' and the 'editor' to the discussion on ends and means in the following chapter (Chapter XVI). Gandhi is of the opinion that good ends could be achieved only through moral means. Petitioning the government was a way of educating the people while articulating the grievances of the Indians.

The time has come for petition to be backed by force, moral force. If the British government refuses to entertain or look into our petitions we should refuse to cooperate with it, because, as sums up Gandhi, 'the force of arms is powerless when matched against the force of love and soul.'[21]

(c) India can win independence through passive resistance

Chapter XVII is devoted to the further elaboration of 'the force of love and soul' represented through 'passive resistance'.[22] The chapter begins with the reader expressing doubts regarding the success of soul force because, he believes, there is no evidence in history to show that soul force has ever succeeded. Gandhi replies that since 'history is really a record of every interruption of the even working of the force of love and soul[23] therefore there is little reference to the working of soul force there. 'Soul force being natural, is not noted in history.'[24] Gandhi defines passive resistance as a 'method of securing rights by personal suffering; it is the reverse of resistance by arms. When I refuse to do a thing that is repugnant to my conscience, I use soul force.'[25] Gandhi proceeds to draw a distinction between the laws made by the legislatures or human institutions and laws of the conscience which, according to him, are any day better than man made laws. Similarly he considers it a 'superstition and ungodly thing to believe that an act of a majority binds a minority[26] alluding to the accepted procedure for making of laws by the legislatures. The reader is still not clear about the potent weapon of passive resistance which he believes is a good weapon for the weak while the strong can take up arms. Gandhi reprimands him for his ignorance and tells him that passive resistance requires greater courage than what is required in taking up arms though a physically weak person can also be a passive resister. 'Control over the mind is alone necessary, when that is attained, man is free like the king of the forest and his very glance withers the enemy'.[27]

A passive resister needs to follow a strict discipline of the body and the mind. He has to follow, under all circumstances, the vows of chastity, of remaining in poverty, truthfulness, and last but not least, fearlessness. Passive resistance, according to Gandhi, is a double edged sword; it morally uplifts the resister and at the same time also conquers the enemy. Gandhi states that whenever people had refused to obey the unjust orders of their rulers in India in the past, they practised passive resistance.

(d) Importance of education in swaraj

Gandhi had always been a great supporter of proper education. His discussion of *swarajya* would have been incomplete without a discussion on education. Hence in Chapter XVIII he discusses the importance of education. He criticizes the British system of primary education that focuses on three R's which Gandhi believes is irrelevant for an Indian peasant. Gandhi also considers higher education imparted in India to be worthless because it does not deal with or teach the student values of life. The 'reader' is understandably disturbed by these views and counters Gandhi by saying that it is only because he is educated he has been able to form opinions on such diverse subjects. Gandhi patiently tells him that he is not against knowledge of letters but what he wants to emphasize is that one should not make a fetish of education.

Real education is about character building. It should include knowledge of a language apart from our provincial language such as Sanskrit for Hindus, Arabic for Muslims and Persian for Parsees. Hindi in the *Devanagari* script should be the link language. English language should be given up 'Is it not a sad commentary that we should have to speak of Indian Home Rule in a foreign language?' [28]

(e) *Machinery should not replace human labour*

Chapter XIX is the most controversial chapter of the book wherein Gandhi criticizes machines. He is of the opinion that machines have impoverished India. The Manchester mills, by supplying cheap cloth to India, have made the Indian weavers lose their jobs and livelihood. The mill owners in India also have a vested interest in this and because of their support the British are continuing to exploit Indians. Gandhi further widens criticism of machinery by including a criticism of tram cars, electricity and printing presses in it but fails to give a very convincing argument in support of his views.

(f) Gandhi's definition of swaraj

In the last chapter the 'reader' concludes that since the views of Gandhi do not match those of either the extremists or moderates perhaps he represents a third party. Gandhi disagrees with the description because he does not believe in any kind of partisanship but specifies his differences with the 'Extremist' and the 'Moderates'. He disagrees with the 'Extremists' with regard to the use of brute force and asks the 'Moderates' to back their petition with the force of soul in order to make them effective.

Gandhi pleads to British government that it follow the Indian civilization if it wishes to remain in India and asks it to desist from spending money on railway and military, and replace Hindi with English as a language of instruction in education. If these conditions are not met, Gandhi suggests that it would not be possible for Indians to co-operate with the British. Gandhi also enumerates a list of 19 conditions regarding how he wanted people to conduct themselves in order to obtain real *swaraj*. This list includes instructions to lawyers, doctors, wealthy people on how to make themselves useful for their country and countrymen. There is also a curious instruction (No.17) which states that one 'should understand that deportation for life to Andamans is not enough expiation for the sin of encouraging European civilization.' This is probably a hint to those who propagated violent means for attaining independence for India because the point immediately preceding it emphasizes self suffering, and the point succeeding this one, sings the virtue of passive resistance and self suffering involved in it.

The 'reader' is alarmed at the ambitious list and calls it a tall order. Gandhi, however, is uncompromising. He states that real home rule is self rule or *self control*; which could be *achieved only through passive resistance*; which *requires the use of swadeshi*; and this could be achieved *not by hating the English but by convincing them that their rule of taxes, unnecessary expenditures, etc was harmful.*

He winds up the discussion on *swaraj* by stating unequivocally 'my conscience testifies that my life henceforth is dedicated to its attainment'. And Gandhi did exactly this in his life-time.

How this small booklet was received by the general public, Indian leaders, public figures, writers and philosophers and the British rulers during Gandhi's life-time, forms an interesting account which shall be discussed in due course. What is important at this point is to state that though Gandhi was in the thick of the struggle for the rights of the Indian community in South Africa, Indian independence was not farther from his mind and he was almost prophetic about his vision of the strategy to be followed to win independence for India.

REFERENCES

1. Rajmohan Gandhi writes that Gandhi was able to influence only three of these, V.V.S. Aiyar, Asaf Ali and T.S.S. Rajan who supported Gandhi's movements in India. *Mohandas*, Penguin, Delhi, 2006, p. 150.
2. M.K. Gandhi, *Hind Swaraj*, Navajivan Press, Ahmedabad, 2005, p. 40.
3. This approach is similar to the approach followed by Plato in his book the *Republic* where Socrates in his discussion on justice examines first what justice in not. Similar tradition is found in the *Upanishads* where *brahma* is sought in the quest of *neti neti iti brahamah* 'not this, not this, this is *brahmah*'.
4. p. 30.
5. p. 34.
6. p. 37.

7. p. 37.
8. p. 38.
9. p. 40.
10. Badrinath (North), Shringeri (South), Puri (East), and Dwarka (West)
11. p. 43.
12. p. 44.
13. p. 46.
14. p. 46.
15. p. 52.
16. p. 53.
17. p. 59.
18. After the 1857 war of independence the Indians were not permitted to carry arms.
19. p. 59.
20. p. 60.
21. p. 66.
22. Gandhi had already chosen the term 'satyagraha' over 'passive resistance' for his movement in South Africa in 1906. Since the term satyagraha was not in common use at the time of the writing of *Hind Swaraj* he continues to use the term 'passive resistance' but the content of passive resistance he promotes in *Hind Swaraj* is the same as that of satyagraha though Gandhi differentiated between the two in his other writings.
23. p. 68.
24. p. 68.
25. p. 69.
26. p. 70.
27. p. 71.
28. p. 78.

PART–III

COMMENTARIES ON *HIND SWARAJ* AND GANDHIAN THOUGHT

To be true to my faith, therefore, I may not write in anger or malice. I may not write idly. I may not write merely to excite passion. The reader can have no idea of the restraint I have to exercise from week to week in the choice of topics and my vocabulary. It is training for me. It enables me to peep into myself and to make discoveries of my weaknesses. Often my vanity dictates a smart expression or my anger a harsh adjective. It is a terrible ordeal but a fine exercise to remove these weeds.

—M.K. Gandhi
Young India, July 2, 1925

6
Anthony J Parel's Commentary on *Hind Swaraj*

I read your book with great interest because I think that the question you treat in it – the passive resistance – is a question of the greatest importance not only for India but for the whole humanity.

– Leo Tolstoy's letter to Gandhi (8th May, 1910), on reading Hind Swaraj.

Anthony J. Parel, Professor of Emeritus of Political Science at the University of Calgary, was entrusted by John Dunn of Kings College, Cambridge and Geoffrey Hawthorn, Faculty of Social and Political Science, University of Cambridge, to contribute to their series of *Cambridge Texts in Modern Politics*.. The intention of this series was to familiarize the students studying in the Universities of Europe and Americas with the movements of national liberation in Latin America, Africa and Asia, which may not be derivatives of Western ideologies or idioms. Anthony J Parel chose to write a commentary on *Hind Swaraj,* Gandhi's most representative and original work.

In the introduction to this work, *Hind Swaraj and Other Writings* (1997) Parel describes in brief the importance of *Hind Swaraj* for a correct understanding of Gandhi's thought. He elaborates upon the intentions that were behind Gandhi's writing of the book, some of which Gandhi has himself indicated in the foreword of the book, and others which Parel gleans from his various writings spread over different periods of time. Parel also explores the historical roots of Gandhi's thought in the idea of modern civilization that was being discussed at the time when Gandhi wrote *Hind Swaraj*. Similarly, the impact of South African politics, the politics of expatriate Indians, and the Indian national movement are also treated as historical contexts for the writing of *Hind Swaraj* by Parel. Since *Hind Swaraj* is not only a historical reference but also a philosophical one, the intellectual roots of Gandhian thought are traced by Parel in the western sources like his legal training, brush with Christianity, and his readings of the works of Plato, Tolstoy, Ruskin, Emerson and other leading lights of the western intellectual tradition. Apart from the western sources, the indigenous roots of Gandhi's intellectual makeup are also explored extensively by Parel.

The structure of the book is analysed while discussing its literary genre. Most importantly, Parel discusses at length the reception the book got when it was first published and whenever it was discussed later. Last but not least, the contemporary influence of the booklet is also examined to emphasize its continued relevance.

Addressed to Whom

There were four categories of people to whom *Hind Swaraj* was addressed: expatriate Indians, 'Extremists' and 'Moderates' of the Indian National Congress, the Indian nation and the English.

Intention

As to why Gandhi wrote the book, Parel gives six reasons:

- Gandhi had been continuously thinking about it and when he got inner enlightenment he could not restrain himself from communicating his ideas to others.
- Gandhi wanted to clarify the concept of swaraj by distinguishing between 'swaraj as self-government or the quest for home rule or good state, and swaraj as self rule or the quest for self-improvement'.
- Gandhi was disturbed by the misguided Indians residing outside India who thought that they could win India's independence through violent means.

- He wanted to show to Indians that modern civilization which had kept them under its spell was more dangerous than colonialism. He wanted to bring out a reconciliation between the English and the Indians because deluded by modern civilization they were treating each other as their enemies.
- Through *Hind Swaraj* Gandhi wanted the Indians to become acquainted with the new concept of *dharma* that would be more appropriate for them in the modern age.

Historical Context

After enumerating the intentions of Gandhi in writing *Hind Swaraj*, Parel takes up the discussion of the historical context of the book, *Hind Swaraj*.

According to Parel 'Modern civilization forms the broad historical context of Hind Swaraj. Its critique of that civilization is one of its main contributions to modern political thought.'

Gandhi's discussion of modern civilization is 'critical' not 'negative' asserts Parel. Being critical means that there is an innate desire to improve the object criticized. Gandhi lauds some of the achievements of modern civilization but this appreciation is conditional in the sense that the contributions have to be combined with others in order to make them truly beneficial eg., rights to go with duties and empirical knowledge with moral insights.

Modern civilization, according to Gandhi came as a result of Enlightenment in Europe and was felt more with the coming of Industrial Revolution. The latter changed not only the means of production but also brought about changes in the way of thinking. Politics came to be separated from morality; economic prosperity became its goal. The attitude towards religion and towards physical work changed.

Liberal political theory distinguished between industrialized nations and non-industrial nations. The former were considered fit for democracy and the latter for authoritarian rule or colonial government. Because of their disunity and internal hostilities the latter were not considered qualified to rule over themselves. The most vocal representative of this viewpoint was an Englishman named James Fitzjames Stephen (1829-94) who expressed these views in his essay, 'Foundations of the government of India'. Parel is of the opinion that it is 'in the context of arguments such as Stephen's that Gandhi develops his critique of modern civilization.'

The politics of South Africa where Gandhi spent twenty-one years of his early adult life is another historical context examined by Parel. Parel writes 'it was in South Africa, not in India, that he first acquired a vision of Indian nationhood.' Gandhi learnt that 'he was first an Indian, then a Gujarati, and only then a Kathiawadi.' According to Parel, the following issues related to Gandhi's relationship with South Africa need to be highlighted.

1. '...it was in South Africa that Gandhi for the first time became aware that modern civilization was at the root of the colonial problem'. As a proof Parel cites the after-dinner speech delivered by Gandhi on Christmas day in 1896 and again at a lecture delivered in 1908 before a YMCA audience in which he associated modern civilization with force and of being centrifugal in nature and therefore without a goal.
2. South Africa offered 'relative social freedom' to Gandhi to conduct his social and political experiments for India. The Indian community in South Africa was free from the evils of communalism, regionalism, casteism and male -domination that plagued the community in India.
3. Gandhi's lobbying missions of 1906 and 1909 to London helped him acquire the diplomatic skill necessary for dealing with the British political establishment and also acquainted him with the expatriate Indians.
4. Gandhi came into direct touch with Indians fighting for the freedom of their country from outside India. With regard to the latter, Parel writes: 'These were

> the new converts to modern civilization, and it is their uncritical acceptance of their newly found secular faith that really bothered Gandhi. Modern civilization was bad enough for Britain, but when imported into India and propagated there by Indians themselves, its potential for mischief became incalculable.'[1]

The second area explored by Parel under the head historical context is the politics of expatriate Indians. Most of these were students or graduates who had gone abroad and were living mostly in England, United States, Canada, different parts of Europe and even Japan. Disenchanted with the lack of success of the Moderates in the Congress these people were drawn to the European revolutionary movements and ideas like terrorism, Russian nihilism, Marxism, the ideologies of the Irish Home Rule movement and Italian *Risorgimento.*

The most important of the expatriate Indians was Shyamji Krishnavarma, a Gujarati linguist who was working as an assistant to the famous Oxford Sanskritist, Sir Monier- Monier Williams. A qualified barrister, Krishnavarma worked under maharajas for some time in India before returning to England to devote full time to Indian national movement. He started scholarships for Indian students studying abroad, founded the India House (1905) and started a revolutionary penny monthly, *The Indian Sociologist.* His activities became suspect and he shifted to Paris in 1907. He also inspired revolutionaries like VD Savarkar who was the inspiration behind Madan Lal Dhingra's act of assassination of Curzon–Wyllie in 1909.Gandhi had the opportunity of sharing with Savarkar a platform in 1909 and the difference between their respective approaches became clear when they 'agreed to disagree on the question of whether the *Ramayana* taught *ahimsa* or not'. Other revolutionaries who were slightly of the communist / socialist hue were Madame Bhikaji Rustom Cama, V. Chattopadhyaya and Lala Hardayal.

Influenced by Krishnavarma was Taraknath Das, a former member of Bengal secret society, *Anusilan Samiti,* who started a penny monthly in Canada known as *Free Hindustan* after the fashion of *The Indian Sociologist.* It was in this monthly that Tolstoy's *Letter to a Hindoo* was published, in which Tolstoy had criticized the methods followed by terrorists .This letter was sent to Gandhi by one of his friends and after getting it authenticated by Tolstoy, Gandhi translated it at the same time when he was writing the *Hind Swaraj.* Taraknath Das and V. Chattopadhyaya both had in their individual capacities refuted the arguments put forward by Tolstoy whereas Gandhi defended and supported Tolstoy.

The Indian National Movement was another historical context to the writing of *Hind Swaraj.* Parel is of the opinion that the Indian national movement 'occasioned the fundamental debate on the nature of her national identity, which in some ways continues even today.' Gandhi did not accept the reading of national identity as represented by Tilak through Ganapati or Shivaji festivals because of their Hindu bias and also did not agree with Aurobindo's appeal to *shakti* because of the inherent violent nature of the idea. The ideas put forward by the Moderates about the economic drain of the wealth of India by the British were found more appealing to him because his nationalism included the poor, the common man. (See also his views in the chapter on Italy). Having closely worked with the Muslims in South Africa for the cause of the Indian community the idea of excluding them from Indian nation was an anathema for Gandhi, thus a full chapter on Hindu-Muslim question in the *Hind Swaraj.*

Philosophical Context

Since *Hind Swaraj* is not only a historical reference it is also a philosophical reference it is important to trace the intellectual context in which it was written. Parel divides the intellectual context between western sources and Indian sources. Parel treats the books listed by Gandhi in the appendix to *Hind Swaraj,* as philosophical sources.

The first western influence on Gandhi could be the legal studies that he pursued in England in 1888. Parel is of the opinion that this training 'deepened in him the idea of a higher law morally superior to any constitution and positive law.' This was also one of the reasons that his approach to politics was 'as much jurisprudential as ethical'.

Gandhi's contact with the Vegetarian Society of London and the writers associated with it reconfirmed Gandhi s faith in the vegetarian way of life as not only a fad but with deep philosophical implications. Howard Williams, an eminent vegetarian, had written in his book *The Ethics of Diet* (1881) that vegetarians were pioneers of a 'truer civilization' and exploded the myth that vegetarianism was the cause of the defeat of Hindus at the hands of beef-eating foreigners. Parel points out that Gandhi's critique of modern medicine and modern doctors in Chapter XII of *Hind Swaraj* becomes intelligible in this context as being related to modern civilization.

From his contact with Christians and the reading of the Christian texts Gandhi was inspired to devote his life to service of humanity and learning the skills like farming, carpentry, shoe-making, bookbinding, printing and baking, and also organizing life in ashrams around such activities.

Gandhi's brush with Greek literature was through Plato's *Apology*. Parel believes that 'The major lesson he learnt from this book, a lesson which was to find its way to *Hind Swaraj*, was that there was an irrefragable moral link between the order in the soul and the order in the society. Of equal importance was the doctrine of the ultimacy of the inner conscience and the option to suffer harm rather than inflict it.' According to Gandhi Socrates was a great 'satyagrahi'.

It was the Russian writer and philosopher Leo Tolstoy who seems to have the deepest influence on Gandhi. Gandhi goes to the extent of directing his readers to read at least four books by Tolstoy mentioned in the appendix to *Hind Swaraj*. These cover four broad topics: Christianity as an ethical religion; aesthetics and political action; critique of the new industrial civilization and the colonial question of India.

Tolstoy's book *The Kingdom of God is within You* makes a case for Christianity as an ethical religion rather than a dogma. Tolstoy claims to have found the answer to the question of violence through the reading of the New Testament. In order to resolve violence resulting from the contrary view held by the opponent, Tolstoy holds that either one must find 'an absolute and indubitable criterion of evil' or one must not 'resist evil by violence. Tolstoy acknowledges that this belief is not supported by institutional Christianity that believes in the concept of a just war. This view is also not acceptable to modern social scientists, who do not believe in the concept of conscience. The modern social scientists assume that once material inequalities were suitably addressed, violence would automatically go.[2] Tolstoy is of the opinion that even if external conditions are improved, 'the position of humanity will not be bettered'. It can improve only if both internal and external changes occur, when 'humans learn to listen to their true Christian conscience in which alone is revealed the Kingdom of God, which is the kingdom of love and non-violence.'

Tolstoy's idea of the rejection of the doctrine of autonomous art i.e., art for art's sake also found favour with Gandhi. Like Tolstoy Gandhi too believed in emphasizing the importance of experience and feeling, in religious origins of great art and on the need to communicate feeling through appropriate symbols. Gandhi's insistence on the need to have 'inner experience' of *swaraj* in order to communicate to others in a more credible and authentic manner owes its origin to this relationship between aesthetics and political action.

Tolstoy's other writings listed in the appendix concern themselves with the various drawbacks of the industrial civilization and hence are recommended by Gandhi.

The Letter to a Hindoo, referred to earlier is also an explanation of colonialism in India. Gandhi has borrowed almost verbatim Tolstoy's words that 'it is *not* the English who have enslaved India but the Indians who have enslaved themselves.' Tolstoy believes that what India needs was not revivalism but a practical commitment to non-violence in order to free itself of the colonial yoke and the mindset of servility.

Another writer who had deep influence on Gandhi was John Ruskin. Ruskin's idea of true economy being the proper management of a nation's labour expressed in his book with the telling title *A Joy for ever and its Price in the Market* was the intellectual forerunner of Gandhi's insistence on 'appropriate technology' for India which did not take away the jobs of the workers. From Ruskin's another book *Unto This Last* Gandhi borrowed the concept of 'bread labour' i.e. each and every person, in every situation should earn his/her bread through physical labour as well. Gandhi translated the book under the title *Sarvodaya* and adapted Ruskin's terminology to suit Indian understanding. Thus Ruskin's concept of 'social affection' for human economy was translated as *daya* (compassion), Ruskin's idea of moderating market forces through 'honour' was translated as *satya* (truth) and Ruskin's emphasis on handicrafts along with factories got translated as spinning -wheel for the whole of India. The close link between *Sarvodaya* and *Hind Swaraj* is borne out by the fact that the last chapter of *Sarvodaya,* reads like a prelude to *Hind Swaraj*. Parel writes: 'Gandhi recognized, the Indian middle class was clamouring for *swaraj,* which it identified with political power—to be gained by driving out the British by force—and with economic prosperity—to be brought about by rapid industrialization. Gandhi found such a notion of *swaraj* totally unacceptable....Real *swaraj* required not only political power and economic prosperity but also, and above all, a certain moral development among the people, especially the middle class.'

Gandhi's emphasis on village uplift had its support in the writings of H.S. Maine's classic, *Village Communities in East and West.* Gandhi's idea of modern civilization being a disease was borrowed from Carpenter's *Civilization: Its Cause and Cure* (1889) where the author likened civilization to measles, a stage in the development of human beings. Gandhi was more optimistic. He considered civilization, to quote Parel, as 'a curable disease and Gandhi its doctor.' Blount's pamphlet *The*

Crusade which advocated the use of homemade products, was summarized in *Indian Opinion,* the newspaper edited by Gandhi, anticipated Gandhi's emphasis on home spun khadi. Another book, which was serialized in the newspaper was Taylor's *Fallacy of Speed.* Taylor had argued against the railways for the resultant imbalance it created in urban and rural, social and economic life, and concluded that speed rather than providing leisure to individuals, destroys it. Similarly Max Nordau's books on civilization and its paradoxes, and RH Sherard's *White Slaves of England* – dwell on pessimism as the theme of modern civilization where the rich have grown insensitive to the sufferings of their fellow poor.

The influence of American authors on Gandhi was no less. Henry David Thoreau' *Principles of Civil Disobedience* impressed Gandhi with its contention that conscience was more important than majority decisions. About Emerson's *Essays* that were translated for his newspaper he said that they were 'teaching of Indian wisdom in Western garb.'

A careful reading of these sources suggests that Gandhi attacked the unhealthy tendencies of the Western civilization and guarded even the English against it. Thus his criticism as Parel writes 'was not motivated by any consideration of narrow nationalism or anti-colonialism.'[3]

Parel also treats at length the Indian sources from which Gandhi derived his philosophy. Indian sources are significant because as writes Parel, 'It is Indian philosophical thought that enables Gandhi to integrate the ideas he gathered from the West into a coherent whole.' Gandhi's stay in England where he was pursuing his lawyer's degree, made him aware of his Indian identity and the need to know more and more about it. This quest was at its peak during his South African years where again, Gandhi was supposed to represent the Indians and expected to know all about India. In England Gandhi read Edwin Arnold's translation of the *Gita* (*The Song Celestial*) and the biography of Lord Buddha, *The Light of Asia.* For Gandhi India was not only Hindu India but also a country belonging to the Muslims and people of other faiths. He wanted to be familiar with their philosophy as well and read *The Life of Mahomet and His Successors* by Washington Irving and from *Heroes and Hero Worship* authored by Thomas Carlyle, about the life of the Prophet. He also read about Parsee religion from *The Sayings of Zarathustra* which dealt with the teaching of Zoarashtra, the founder of Parsee religion.

By Gandhi's own account the Indian thinker who was his guide on religion and spiritual affairs and who had the deepest influence on him was Rajchandra Ravjibhai Mehta. He was a Gujarati Jain, mystic and a diamond merchant. When in throes of intellectual crisis Gandhi would consult him especially on the nature of soul (*atma*), God, and liberation (*moksha*) and similar metaphysical, spiritual or ritualistic themes. It is interesting to note that Gandhi was greatly influenced by Rajchandra's interpretation of the Jain doctrine of *anekantavada,* the many-sidedness of religious truth while referring to other religions.

Gandhi's conception of *dharma* also owes its origin to the meaning of *dharma* given by Rajchandra. According to Rajchandra *dharma* did not mean any particular creed or dogma, nor did it mean learning by rote the sacred texts (*Shastras*) or in believing all that they say. Rather *dharma* 'is a quality of the soul' present in every human being through which one knows one's duty in human life and one's true relation with other souls. Dharma was merely a means, (*sadhana*) by which one knows oneself. No organized religion is a special repository of dharma. 'We may accept this means from wherever we get it, whether from India or Europe or Arabia. Gandhi's idea of a 'religion that underlies or religions' discussed in Chapter VIII of *Hind Swaraj,* no doubt comes from Rajchandra's idea.

Apart from Rajchandra, Gandhi was deeply influenced by the teachings of non-attachment enshrined in the *Gita* and the idea of dutifulness and administration in the *Ramacharitmanas*

A wonderful assimilation of all these influences are reflected in the *Hind Swaraj.*

Literary Genre

Parel examines the literary genre of the great booklet as this genre was unique in so far as Gandhi's other writings are concerned. Gandhi put forward his views in the form of dialogue between a 'reader' and an 'editor' to make it an interesting reading as well as amenable to expressing different points of view. Parel holds that Gandhi deliberately avoided making the protagonists *guru* and *shishya* because that would have involved deference on the part of the disciple and thus inhibited frank discussion.

Parel also points out the advantage of a dialogue in not making a discussion final, in the nature of a 'blue print' but leaving it open-ended for further modifications and adaptations which is essential for a true philosophical discussion.

Structure of Hind Swaraj

The book is divided into twenty chapters where up to Chapter XI Gandhi dwells on the historical references. Thereafter he takes up the philosophical issues of defining the meaning of swaraj, discussing the nature of civilization, the use of violence, meaning of dharma and the importance of self -rule as a prerequisite to real home rule.

Reception

The importance of a great work lies in the abiding interest of the readers in it. This is reflected in how the book was initially received and how it is being received till this date. Apart from Tolstoy whose appreciation for the book was unqualified others either criticized it or were neutral to it or gave it conditional support. The British banned it, Gokhale found it impractical; the intellectuals liked some parts of it and dismissed the rest. Now again it is in the limelight.

Influence

Hind Swaraj generally got a hostile reception on its publication. Except for Tolstoy who thought that the book raised the question of passive resistance which was of importance not only to India but to the rest of the world as well; others, however, rejected it as either 'dangerous'(British Government) or 'hastily written'(Gokhale). Krishnavarma considered it as propagating the Christian virtue of suffering, while the need of the hour was to take a proactive stand for the freedom of the country. W.Y. Wyberg, a member of the Transvaal Assembly, South Africa and a theosophist, wrote to Gandhi 'What you call 'soul force' and 'passive resistance' have nothing to do with love or spirituality in themselves. In advocating these things instead of physical force, you are only transferring the battle and violence from the physical to the mental plane. Your weapons are mental and psychic, not physical, but also not spiritual'. M.N. Roy dismissed the book as not taking into consideration the laws of class struggle. Others like Sir Sankaran Nair accused Gandhi of propagating anarchism.

American response to *Hind Swaraj* was positive in nature and it led to the debate on the virtues of decentralization and mass production.

After the unprecedented devastation during the Second World War, *Hind Swaraj* was examined afresh in Europe and some appreciation of Gandhi's ideas came.

In 1945 a huge debate took place on the points raised in the book between Nehru and Gandhi with Nehru disagreeing with Gandhi on most of the points. In 1973 the official journal of Gandhi Peace Foundation organized a symposium on *Hind Swaraj*. While the majority of the participants praised the book, the noted historian R.C. Majumdar was critical of Gandhi's description of modern civilization and his stand on the Hindu-Muslim question. In 1985 Nageshwar Prasad published *Hind Swaraj: The Fresh Look* which brought the book into focus again.

Contemporary Influence

Towards the end of his essay Parel recounts the influence of *Hind Swaraj* on contemporary movements, people and thinking. Two important movements in India, the *Bhoodan* , 'gift of land' movement of Vinoba Bhave and the bringing into the mainstream the dacoits of central India by the power of love, a movement led by Jayaprakash Narayan, were inspired by Gandhi. Similarly Gandhi was the inspiration behind the civil rights movement of Martin Luther king in USA in the 1960s.

Hind Swaraj also established Gandhi's credentials as a thinker and a theoretician. The intellectual discussions enshrined in the book are considered as an authentic explanation of colonialism, by Bhikhu Parekh and Ashis Nandy in India. It is the inspiration behind various 'conflict resolution studies' by scholars throughout the world.

As a text it occupies an important place in the study of comparative political thought and is unique in integrating Indian philosophy with the discussion on civilization. It gives a new meaning to the concept of liberty with the use of the term Swaraj, a multilayered concept meaning self-rule as well as inner freedom or positive freedom. Not only that, Parel emphasizes the fact that Gandhi reinstates into political philosophy the relation between self-realization and politics thereby demonstrating the power of one man and in this context *Hind Swaraj* is both a spiritual and a practical book.

A discerning reader would note how Anthony Parel has used the insights provided by both Quentin Skinner and Terence Ball along with his own interventions to highlight the hitherto lesser known aspects of *Hind Swaraj*. Parel unravels the inspiration behind the thoughts of Gandhi as expressed in the book other than those specifically mentioned by Gandhi. He gives due importance to the list of readings mentioned at the end of the booklet to make sense of what Gandhi wanted to say. This approach has helped a great deal in reading and understanding *Hind Swaraj*.

REFERENCES

1. p. xxiv.
2. Perhaps Tolstoy was alluding to the socialist thinking on this matter.
3. p. xlvii.

Chart Showing Summary of Anthony Parel's Views

Anthony J. Parel: Hind Swaraj and other Writings
INTRODUCTION

I – GANDHI'S INTENTIONS

(a) Inner Illumination and consequent Urge to communicate
(b) To clarify the meaning of Swaraj
(c) To respond to the Ideology of Terrorism
(d) To teach Indians that Modern Civilization was more dangerous than colonialism
(e) To contribute towards reconciliation of Indians and Britions
(f) To give Indians an updated conception of 'Dharma' that would fit them for life in the Modern World

II – HISTORICAL CONTEXT

(a) Modern Civilization—Epistemological Consequences
(b) Politics of South Africa—Objective Vision, Critical Outsider
(c) Politics of Expatriate Indians—Disenchantment with Moderates
(d) Indian National Movement—Dabate On National Identity

III – INTELLECTUAL CONTEXT

Western Sources

1. Legal Training
2. Vegetarianism–H. Williams
3. Chritianity–Service
4. Plato
5. Tolstoy, Ruskin, Emerson

Indian Sources

1. The Gita
2. Rajchandra
3. Tulsidas' Ramacharitamanas

IV – LITERARY GENRE

1. Dialogue
2. Chapters. I to XI Historical Reference
3. Chapters–XII to XX Philosophical References

V – RECEPTION

Tolstoy–British Government
Shyamji Krishnavarma
Wyberg
Gokhale
Aryan Path (1938)

VI – CONTEMPORARY INFLUENCE

1. Vinoba Bhave, JP
2. B. Parekh, A. Nandy (Colonial)
3. Lanza Del Vesto, M. Luther King
4. Gene Sharp (Strategy)
5. Erik Erikson (Psy.)
6. Others

7

Concept of Satyagraha with Special Reference to Bhikhu Parekh's views

My study and experience of non-violence have proved to me that it is the greatest force in the world. It is the surest method of discovering the truth and it is the quickest because there is no other. It works silently, almost imperceptibly, but none the less surely. It is the one constructive process of Nature in the midst of incessant destruction going on about us. I hold it to be a superstition to believe that it can work only in private life. There is no department of life public or private to which that force cannot be applied. But this non-violence is impossible without complete self-effacement.

Mahatma Gandhi's message to 'World Tomorrow, a magazine published from New York, USA, for its 'Gandhi Number' published in 1924, CWMG, Vol. XXV, pp. 323-24.

Satyagraha

Satyagraha Explained

One of the most important contributions of Gandhi to political thought has been his theory of *satyagraha.* The word satyagraha was coined in the midst of the Indian community's movement of passive resistance in South Africa (1906) when Gandhi was looking for an appropriate word to describe his struggle in order to emphasize its moral content. Gandhi wanted to distinguish his movement from the contemporary passive resistance movement of Suffragettes in England which was very aggressive and at times violent too. He also wanted to use an Indian expression to describe a movement carried out by Indians. He asked the readers of his newspaper, *Indian Opinion,* to suggest a suitable word and finally zeroed in on the word *sadagraha* suggested by Maganlal Gandhi. He modified the word and finally decided to call his fight for justice as *satyagraha.* Giving reasons for his choice Gandhi later wrote:

> I liked the word, but it did not fully represent the whole idea I wished to connote. I therefore corrected it to *satyagraha.* Truth (*satya*) implies love, and firmness (*agraha*) engenders and therefore serves as a synonym of force. I thus began to call the Indian movement "*satyagraha*" that is to say, the force that is born to Truth and Love or non-violence, and gave up the phrase "passive resistance"...

As we know Gandhi continued to use the phrase 'passive resistance' as in *Hind Swaraj* (published in 1909) because the people the world over were more familiar with the term than they were with *satyagraha.* In *Hind Swaraj* he uses the term passive resistance as a synonym for *satyagraha.*

Gandhi's preference for the term satyagraha over passive resistance is clear when we see how he distinguished between the two terms in his book *Satyagraha in South Africa* (first published in 1925):

- *(a)* The word 'passive' hints at weakness because of it not being an 'active' resistance to evil.
- *(b)* Love is the essential ingredient of *satyagraha* whereas it is missing in passive resistance.
- *(c)* Physical force though not used, is not ruled out in passive resistance whereas *satyagraha* is totally non-violent.
- *(d)* Satyagraha can be even offered to one's near and dear ones whereas passive resistance can be offered only when the other party ceases to be our near or dear one.
- *(e)* Harassment or injury to opponent is completely ruled out in *satyagraha.*

(*f*) Though self-suffering is common in both passive resistance and *satyagraha* not all passive resistance movements follow it.

Satyagraha is a Sanskrit word comprising two words—*satya*, that is 'truth' and *agraha* which means 'holding on'. Thus *satyagraha* literally means holding on to the 'truth'. Gandhi's grandson, Rajmohan Gandhi has rightly commented in this connection, 'Using truth as the synonym for love, justice and the soul, and equating firmness with force, Gandhi would allow 'satyagraha' to be translated into English as truth-force, or love-force or soul-force.'[1]

Gandhi used the term to denote his fight against all forms of injustices—social, political, economic or even personal. Satyagraha could be resorted to by one person, (individual *satyagraha*), or it could be a movement carried out by a group or masses.

The rules of *satyagraha*, had to be followed in all kinds of satyagraha. The *satyagrahi* was expected to be truthful, free of hatred for the enemy, non-violent even in the face of all kinds of provocations and fearless in face of danger, including the threat to his or her life as well. The *strategy of satyagraha* involved: informing the other party the issues on which satyagraha could be resorted to; being open to discussions or dialogue with the opposite party; in the event of failure of discussions resorting to non-cooperation and civil disobedience to authority. Fasting was also recommended in rarest of cases but not all satyagrahis were eligible to go on fast.

Satyagraha ranged from purificatory or penitential devices like pledges, prayers and fasts to modes of non-cooperation like *hartal*, boycott, strikes, fasting unto death, *hijrat;* or picketing, marches, non-payment of taxes and deliberate defiance of a specific law.

Since all these measures seemed negative in nature Gandhi instructed that they should be supplemented with Constructive Programme which in the Indian context meant working towards communal harmony, removal of untouchability, adult education, village improvement, peasant uplift and development of non-violent labour unions, decentralized economic development through development of cottage industries and finally, the abolition of various social evils.

Gandhi also emphasized the fact that the powerful weapon of *satyagraha* was not to be used indiscriminately. He continuously wrote about the *conditions and circumstances in which satyagraha could be resorted to* :

- *(a)* It could be resorted to only for a just cause;
- *(b)* It should be absolutely nonviolent in thought, word and deed:
- *(c)* It involves willing obedience to laws or rules that do not go against one's conscience;
- *(d)* *Satyagrahis* should have capacity and willingness to suffer;
- *(e)* Discipline in all ranks was absolutely necessary;
- *(f)* *Satyagrahi* should be an epitome of humility;
- *(g)* *Satyagraha* can be offered only for public good not for personal gain;
- *(h)* Only persons of sterling character should resort to *satyagraha.*

Gandhi led or guided several satyagrahas during his lifetime. The most famous of these were his movements in South Africa for the rights of the Indian community living there.[2] In India Gandhi successfully led the local *satyagrahas* of Champaran in Bihar against the exploitation of indigo farmers by their contractors (1917), the farmers satyagraha in Kheda in 1918 and the Ahmedabad Mill workers strike in the same year. His national movements of Non-cooperation (1920) and Civil Disobedience (1930) are well known. Gandhi also led *satyagraha* against the Communal award in 1932 which granted separate electorate to the so called untouchables. Gandhi's fasts unto death for this cause, and later for communal harmony, are well-documented.

BHIKHU PAREKH'S VIEWS

Prof. Bhikhu Parekh, Professor of Political Theory at the University of Hull, UK, is considered an authority on Gandhi.

Prof Parekh has examined critically the various aspects of Gandhi's political philosophy in great depth and with deep understanding and has written a brilliant book on Gandhi[3] which deals with Gandhi's life and philosophy. In this book he discusses the Gandhian view of *satyagraha* from a perspective that is not usually highlighted. Parekh has critically examined the theory of *satyagraha,* its philosophical roots and innovative nature and also how well that theory can be applied in the imperfect world in which we live.

Gandhi was aware of the limits of rationality and violence:

Prof Parekh begins his description of Gandhi's views on *satyagraha* by examining the *limits of rationality and violence in struggles against injustice.*

According to Prof Parekh, Gandhi rejected the conventional methods of conflict resolution or fighting against injustice. These were either the rational method or the method of body force involving violence. Gandhi, according to Parekh, found "both methods unsatisfactory in varying degrees, and explored one that relied on hitherto untapped 'soul force' or 'truth force.'

Rational method was not very effective because it ignored the fact that one can never be convinced by arguments alone if the heart is biased or if one lacks the motive to accept the argument of the other.

Gandhi was against violence because *violence denied the ontological fact that all human beings had souls a*nd therefore were capable of appreciating and pursuing good. He opposed violence also because, as Parekh puts it, 'The consequences of violence were irreversible in the sense that a life once terminated or damaged could never be revived or easily put together. And irreversible deeds required infallible knowledge to justify them, which was obviously beyond human reach"

Gandhi *rejected violence on moral grounds* as well. Morality consisted in doing what was right because one *believed* it to be right, and required unity of belief and conduct. Since the use of violence did not change the opponent's perception of truth, it compelled him to behave in a manner contrary to his sincerely held beliefs, and violated his moral integrity. Violence also *rarely achieved lasting results* and *had a tendency of inflationary spiral*, subsequently raising the threshold of violence.

Gandhi's *emphasis on the organic relationship between ends and means also ruled out violence to achieve noble ends.*

For Gandhi Soul Force was a Better Alternative than Rationality or Violence

Since both rationality and violence had limited use in struggles against injustice, Gandhi believed that a new method was required. The new method should be able to activate the nobleness of the soul. It should appeal to one's rationality as well as one's emotions. It should be capable of creating an environment free of hatred and conducive to peace where both the parties trust each other. Gandhi was convinced that only *satyagraha* met all these requirements.

There is a chance of converting even the worst criminal to reason because as a human being he too has a soul and is capable of love. The only difference is that his love is limited to his family or dear ones. The goal of the *satyagrahi* should be to find ways of expanding this love.

Satyagraha believed in having a *dialogue with the opponent* so as to understand his point of view and also to try to convince him through argument or persuasion, to understand the *satyagrahi's* point of view as well. If the opponent did not respond in the manner expected by the *satyagrahi,* he should show patience and not harass, embarrass or frighten the opponent. Rather a *satyagrahi* should operate from the hope that his efforts are bound to start in his opponent a voluntary process of self-examination. The moment signs of thaw were found in the opponent's stand all struggle should be suspended so that a hospitable climate for talks is generated.

In order to hold society together it was essential to bear in mind that all human beings had similar humanity in them and the use of *violence against one harmed not only the victim but also the perpetrator of violence as it dehumanized him as well.* Therefore for the collective good of the society violence was not allowed.

Satyagraha was a serious matter and had to be *conducted on the basis of moral principles* such as careful study of situation; patient gathering of facts; reasoned defense of objectives; popular agitation to convince the opponent of the intensity of the *satyagrahi's* feelings and an ultimatum to give him a last chance of negotiation. The channels of communication between both sides were always kept open and intermediaries were encouraged to resolve conflicts. On his part, the *satyagrahi* had to be nonviolent and neither retaliate violence nor resist confiscation of his property if it so happens. He is also supposed to conduct himself well as a prisoner.

Gandhi believed that the element of *voluntary suffering* on the part of the *satyagrahi* is capable of melting the heart of the opponent but Prof Parekh is of the opinion that since all the satyagrahis did not have the moral fibre of Gandhi this did not happen and Gandhi had to supplement his satyagraha with other forms of pressure such as economic boycott, non-payment of taxes etc. Parekh also believes that even Gandhi's vocabulary became more aggressive in the face of an impasse.

Prof Parekh is also critical of fasting as a method of pressurizing the opponent to accede to one's demand. Gandhi was aware of the fact that fasting could be resorted as moral blackmail in the hands of unscrupulous or misguided elements and put strict and almost impossible conditions on those who wanted to use it as a method of satyagraha. Most of the time Gandhi himself resolved to go on fast and did not allow others to do so.

The Limits of Satyagraha: Parekh

Parekh hails Gandhi's theory of satyagraha as a 'highly original and creative contribution to the theories of social change and political action', though he does not believe *satyagraha* to be panacea for all the ills in society. He points out several limitations of *satyagraha*. Parekh holds that Gandhi was wrong in believing that all or even most social conflicts could be resolved by touching the opponent's hearts. Conflicts sometimes occur because there are times when people genuinely believe that their belief is right such as on issues like war, abortion etc. Parekh also contends that though the suffering of the other human being generally moves people, but if they are convinced that the other deserves to suffer their attitude may be different.

Satyagraha is not infallible. A serious limitation of *satyagraha* is that it is dependent on publicity. In a society like that of the Nazis where people were eliminated without a trace, there could have been no opportunity of offering *satyagraha*. . 'Without witness there could be no martyrdom' Parekh agrees with Martin Buber. Hence, without publicity *satyagraha* would have had limited or no impact.

On the question of violence too Parekh seems to differ from Gandhi. He contends that violence may not necessarily be accompanied by ill-will. (This position however is not very different from Gandhi's who preferred violence to cowardice and allowed killing for compassion). Towards the end of the discussion on *satyagraha,* Parekh concedes that in spite of its limitations Gandhi's methods have inspired movements throughout the world 'King's civil rights movement showed both the universal relevance of Gandhi's *satyagraha* and the need for its creative adaptation and development.'

After going through the discussion on the theory and practice of *satyagraha* one can safely say that *satyagraha* is the most misused concept of Gandhi. All kinds of protest movements are given the name *satyagraha* today. Khushwant Singh while writing about the fast by Mamta Bannerjee for Singur farmers said that it was not a *satyagraha* as described by Ms Bannerjee because other avenues of settling disputes had not been explored. Similarly the well known jurist AG Noorani argued in his article in the *Hindustan Times* that when the people's representatives themselves make laws which are accepted as constitutional by the courts, then the same representatives do not have the right to oppose them publicly outside legislature. This is misuse of the term satyagraha.

In spite of its misuse there have been successful instances of *satyagraha* in India and abroad. In the US the civil rights movement of the Blacks was a *satyagraha* and it was successful. In India the Chipko movement of Garhwal region for environmental protection was a *satyagraha*.

The *satyagrahi* of today may not always be a pious, lonely figure. The satyagrahis of today can be seen at peace runs, bicycle yatras for communal harmony, motorbike rallies for Indo-Pak peace and organizing campaigns against female foeticide. They may be seen taking Gandhi films and discussion groups to schools and colleges, radio programmes and wall newspapers to slums and villages or holding comic book workshops and round table discussions with leaders of all political hues, including advocates of terrorism "because everyone deserves to be heard."[4] The profile of satyagrahis of today ranges from Engineer Sandeep Pande who used satyagraha for fair Public Distribution System, Right to Information and Rozgar Scheme; Deben Baruah, the reporter from Assam who seeks to tackle the problems of unemployment and terrorism in his State through nonviolent means; Aamna Mirza a student who started an environmental club in her college in Delhi; Bittoo Sondhi a biker who distributed pamphlets against female foeticide in over 100 villages in Punjab; J Kughnandam a graduate from Chennai, who looks for solutions that will make villagers self-reliant by encouraging them to use indigenous natural resources like silk, cotton and banana tree trunks to manufacture cardboard; or students who simply take to walking to save fuel and improve health or save money from ice-cream to create funds for street-kids.[5] All these are shining examples of *satyagraha*. What Joan D.Bondurant said in 1958 holds true even today :

> The most potent legacy Gandhi left to India was the technique of satyagraha. There was in this instrument of

> action, power to effect change. "Satyagraha" had become the cry of all those who felt aggrieved, and popular agitations, however organized and whatever their objective, were widely described as "satayagraha movements". Informed, responsible, and concerned Indians today reflect upon the use and meaning of "satyagraha" with misgivings, yet with hope; with fond memories, and yet with anxiety for the future. - - - The name has been seized upon to describe many forms of opposition to government, and to explain almost any direct social or political action short of organized violence.[6]

If the world is skeptic about the efficacy of *satyagraha* a quote from Gandhi would suffice. He had said "I believe in what Max Muller said years ago, namely, that truth needed to be repeated as long as there were men who disbelieved it."[7] At another occasion he had said, 'I have been practising with scientific precision non-violence and its possibilities for an unbroken period of over fifty years. I have applied it in every walk of life, domestic, institutional, economic and political. I know of no single case in which it has failed. Where it has seemed sometimes to have failed, I have ascribed it to my imperfections. I claim no perfection for myself. But I do claim to be a passionate seeker after Truth, which is but another name for God. In the course of that search, the discovery of non-violence came to me. Its spread is my life mission. I have no interest in living except for the prosecution of that mission. There is no hope for the aching world except through the narrow and straight path of non-violence. Millions like me may fail to prove the truth in their own lives that would be their failure, never of the eternal law.'[8]

REFERENCES

1. Rajmohan Gandhi, *Mohandas*, Viking, 2006, p. 124.
2. The centenary celebrations of his first satyagraha were organized in India and South Africa in September 2006 when our Prime Minister, Dr Manmohan Singh visited South Africa.
3. Bhikhu Parekh, *Gandhi: A Very Short Introduction*, Oxford University Press, 1997.
4. *Outlook*, 11 September, 2006.

5. *Ibid,* Based on profiles in the magazine.
6. Joan D Bondurant, *The Conquest of Violence: The Gandhian Philosophy o f Conflict,* Barnes and Nobles, 1988.
7. *Harijan,* 7-7-1946, p. 212.
8. *Harijan,* 6-7-1940, pp. 185-6.

8
Gandhi's Critique of Modernity

Civilization is that mode of conduct which points out to man the path of duty.

–M.K Gandhi.

Gandhi's seminal work *Hind Swaraj* is a critique of modern civilization. The discussion in the earlier chapters of this book has already covered Gandhi's views on modern civilization followed by how Gandhi's views on modern civilization were received by his contemporaries and colleagues, and, how these views continue to evoke response.

Disturbed by the trend of violence evident in the freedom movement of India in the early part of the twentieth century, Gandhi held modern civilization responsible for this violence. He considered modern civilization as a disease that had stricken both the Indians and the English. As a disease it was curable but he felt that the younger generation was held under the spell of modern civilization and therefore it was very difficult for them to see how it was harming them.

Emphasis on bodily comforts over spiritual development was the hallmark of modern civilization. Modernity's pet theme–rationality–sounded the death-knell of faith and religion. This was further compounded by the introduction of modern medicine and doctors who resorted to the killing of innocent animals for medical experiments, used animal products as components in medicine and, above all, encouraged people to lead immoral and uncontrolled life by assuring them that if they fell sick because of such a life they could be cured by popping some pills. Gandhi also hinted at the historical fact how the British doctors facilitated the establishment of their Empire in India by curing Indian princes of diseases.

The introduction of railways leading to fast movement had its own problems. Frequent travels made people lose their sense of belonging to one place creating a feeling of rootlessness thus killing community bonds. Easy travelling also led to all sorts of people thronging to religious places thus contaminating the sanctity of these places. Earlier, only the devout would undertake arduous pilgrimages. Railways, believed Gandhi, also facilitated the spread of diseases from one city to another. The people worst hit by railways were the villagers. Railway lines facilitated village crops to be sold in urban markets leading to shortage of food in villages and the resultant poverty and deaths there.

The lawyers were another evil product of modern civilization. Lawyers thrived on the disputes of others, which, out of selfish interest, they perpetuated rather than solved. The Hindu-Muslim tension, believed Gandhi, was largely the doing of lawyers who instead of solving communal disputes aggravated them. Lawyers also helped the perpetuation of the British rule in India by sustaining their judicial system which otherwise could not have been manned by the British alone.

The skewed idea of nation, born out of modern civilization, is also attacked by Gandhi. He believed that nations are not co-terminus with religious groups. The followers of different faiths in India belong to the Indian nation. India has been one nation in ancient times and it remains so in the present times as well. Gandhi believed that there was a religion which was above all religions and this religion should be followed by all irrespective of the religious denomination they belong to.

The most controversial area of the Gandhian critique of modern civilization has been his views on machinery. Though

Gandhi somewhat modified his views on machinery later in his life saying that even the human body is a machine and therefore he was not anti-machinery as it was made out to be, the criticisms remain to this day.

The problem with the Gandhian critique of modern civilization is that it is couched in very stark terms. Probably Gandhi wrote in such a tone to present a caricature that would attract attention and that he managed to do. The earlier discussion by AJ Parel shows how Gandhi's book was received in his lifetime.

Three commentaries on Gandhi's critique of modern civilization are given below. All the authors are well-known Gandhian scholars who have done extensive research on Gandhi and have also written books on Gandhi.

BHIKHU PAREKH ON GANDHI'S CRITIQUE OF MODERNITY

Bhikhu Parekh approaches Gandhi's critique of modernity from three angles, which are interconnected and flow from each other. In the order they appear in Gandhi's analysis these are: *human nature, rationality versus faith* and *violent state.*

Bhikhu Parekh examines Gandhi's critique of modernity in the context of the general critique of modernity by European scholars like Mill, Tolstoy, Durkheim, Marx etc.

According to Parekh though Gandhi had the advantage of critiquing modern civilization from both the western and the eastern perspectives, he was more sympathetic to the latter, 'and primarily saw it through the eyes of one of its victims.'

In order to highlight its historical specificity rather than its spatial characteristic Gandhi called it 'modern' instead of 'western' civilization, in the process also indicating that the European people had earlier followed a different civilization.

Human Nature: Lack of self-restraint

At the base of every civilization is its distinct conception of human nature. If human nature is depicted as selfish, the civilization based on it would also have negative traits.

Modern civilization privileged the body over soul. The predominance of body over soul led to two consequences: self-interest and unrestrained self-indulgence. Self-interest led to insensitivity towards the problems of other human beings. Self-indulgence led to more and more production, more consumption of goods than was required, and over-dependence upon machinery thereby resulting in attaching undue importance to it. This led to human beings being reduced to helpless spectators and represented a new kind of slavery 'more comfortable and invidious and therefore more dangerous.'

Modern civilization emphasized speed and hence was always on the move leading to disruption of man's relation with his environment and making him lose his identity in the process. Constant movement also led to loss of sentiment of goodwill and mutual concern therefore community living was made possible only through instilling fear of law.

Enlightened self-interest, which was admired as a quality of liberty in modern civilization, led to selfishness and immorality. It led to centrifugal society rather than a centripetal society. The exploitation of one's fellow beings was built into the very structure of modern civilization. European imperialism was also one of the reflections of this.

Rationality v. Faith: Naïve rationalism

Since modern civilization laid emphasis on scientific methods and rationality, religion and faith had no place in it. According to Gandhi omnipotence of reason was the worst kind of idolatry. Rationalism justified the enslaving of the people of another country in order to civilize them because the imperialists thought that their (the rulers) understanding of things was right.

Rationalism also ignores the fact that people differ from each other in terms of their nature, that is, *swabhava.*

Violent State: Statist culture

Highly centralized modern state was also the product of modern civilization. People with no sense of commonality can be kept together only through a ruthless state hence the domineering state was a necessity. Even democracies suffered from this defect.

Complex response to modernity

Gandhi's response to modern civilization was a complex one. He praised three achievements of modern civilization. These were *(a)* scientific spirit of enquiry; *(b)* understanding the natural world and bringing it under greater human control; *(c)* contribution to the organizational side of life. But this praise was not unqualified.

Gandhi believed that the scientific spirit of enquiry suffered from being defined in 'narrowly positivist and aggressive terms' and extended to 'those areas of life where it was least applicable'. Understanding of the world and bringing it under human control had saved man from deadly diseases and ill health but created in him a 'morbid fear of death.' Organizational life had cultivated civic virtues, respect for rules, subordination of the individual to collective good etc but it reduced morality to enlightened self-interest. By focusing on institutional importance it has left no scope for diversity and freedom of conscience.

Gandhi brought to the critique of modern civilization a perspective not available to its western critics. This also had its disadvantages because though materialist at one level modern civilization also has a moral and spiritual dimension.

DAVID HARDIMAN: 'AN ALTERNATIVE MODERNITY[1]

Hardiman examines *Gandhi's views on modernity as a dialogue between Gandhi and modern civilization.* In this dialogue Gandhi appreciates some features of modern civilization and rejects others. Gandhi supports, for instance, modern concept of human rights, fundamental equality of all humans, the right of all to democratic representation, the principle of governance through persuasion rather than coercion etc. He even goes to the extent of accusing the western governments that they were not following these principles in spirit.

Gandhi, however, criticizes modern civilization for its doctrines of materialism, rationalism, lack of morality, large scale production leading to excessive consumerism and greed, system of medicine aimed at curing rather than preventing diseases, immoral governmental institutions and so on.

Hardiman believes that we commit the error of judging Gandhi by western standards, according to the definition of modernity given by the West. He credits Gandhi with giving an ingenious concept of 'Alternative Modernity', which is neither traditional nor totally in agreement with the western concept, but a constructive critique of modernity accepting its good features.

Gandhi's concept of alternative modernity is reflected in his views mentioned in *Hind Swaraj;* his *idea of civilization* with its preference for arcadian life-style ; his innovative *Constructive Programme*; and, his doctrine of *Trusteeship.* All these ideas have been adequately supported in the West, or outside India as well, and Hardiman gives a detailed account of these.

In *Hind Swaraj* Gandhi criticizes modern civilization for creating an immoral society, by judging progress in terms of technological development aimed at increasing bodily comforts. Hardiman discusses Gandhi's views on railways, doctors, medicine and so on which have already been discussed in the earlier chapters. The alternative modernity of Gandhi comes into play when Gandhi gives his own definition of civilization and asks all to follow that. For him civilization stands for good conduct, doing one's duty and having mastery over mind and passions.

After examining the views expressed in *Hind Swaraj,* Hardiman dwells on the Gandhian *concept of civilization* which reflects a desire to live in 'arcadian simplicity', i.e. a pastoral life close to nature. This, however, did not mean running away from civilization and living in the lap of nature like an ascetic. Nature for Gandhi meant the original or natural form of living, which in many ways, brings man close to natural surroundings as different from urban lifestyle. He wanted to disturb nature only as much as it was absolutely necessary for human existence. This, therefore, was again a new concept close to the present idea of sustainable development and protection of environment.

Hardiman moves on to the description of appropriate technology whereby Gandhi gave his own vision of development in the form of *Constructive Programme.*[2] When Gandhi launched his Non-Co-operation Movement in 1920 he also advocated taking up constructive programme side by side. Constructive Programme included spinning, development of handicrafts, propagating communal unity, movement against untouchability, village uplift and so on. In this programme, Hardiman argues, Gandhi *gave an alternative to the concept of development* with which the West is familiar.He also managed to bring in the distinction between constructive programme and the socialists' concept of development based on class struggle. The latter he held was divisive and violent in nature.

Gandhi was wary of both socialists and capitalists and succeeded in bridging the gap between the two by introducing the theory of *Trusteeship* whereby the capitalists do not exploit the workers for gaining profits. Rather they hold their property as a trust for the welfare of the society. The argument Gandhi gives is that the capitalists owe to the society a debt as in the accumulation of their wealth the society helped them. Both the capitalists and workers should work in harmony and not as class enemies.

Gandhi's Influence outside India

In the last section of his discussion, Hardiman discusses how Gandhi's idea reverberated outside India in different forms. Gandhi's concept of appropriate technology found echo in the idea of 'intermediate technology' developed by Schumacher in his book *Small is Beautiful* published in 1973. Schumacher observed that Gandhi's economic ideas had relevance for developing countries, because, 'as Gandhi said, the poor of the world cannot be helped by mass production but by production by the masses'. The technology that suited them was intermediate technology, which was superior to the primitive technology but at the same time "simpler, cheaper and freer than the super technology of the rich". Apart from Schumacher, Hardiman examines the support for economic ideas of Gandhi in the writings by an Austrian Catholic priest, Ivan Illich. In his book *Tools for Conviviality,* Illich talks about a people-friendly technology and asks society to set limits to growth. In another book *Deschooling Society* Illich takes up the issue of education and like Gandhi, proposes a decentralized and multiple system of learning. In still another book *Medical Nemesis,* Illich echoes Gandhi's concern for modern system of medicine. Lastly in his book *Energy and Equity,* Illich criticizes the present day speedy system of transport as damaging to environment. Here he differs from Gandhi who criticized fast transport as a contributing factor to immorality.

Hardiman also examines how modern developmental strategies do not suit Indian conditions. He quotes the experience of Oxfam workers who sought to implement their method for bringing about the Green Revolution in India and ultimately had to work closely with Gandhian workers adopting their method of work.

Gandhi's longing for rural life is considered to be old fashioned and anti-urban by scholars like Ramachandra Guha. Hardiman defends Gandhi by stating that he was aware of and sensitive to the condition of urban workers as well as was reflected in his speeches and actions during the Ahmedabad Mill workers strike of 1918.

Hardiman winds up his discussion on alternative modernity by referring to the movements for the protection of environment growing lately in India employing Gandhian techniques of nonviolent protest.

POSTMODERN GANDHI

Of late there have been scholars who have described Gandhi as a postmodernist. Nicholas F. Gier, for instance, believes that Gandhi is a 'constructive' postmodernist since he places virtue at the centre of his writings as against the deconstructionist rejection of any central concept.[3]

One to receive maximum attention on this theme, however, has been L.I. Rudolph and S.H. Rudolph's book entitled *Postmodern Gandhi and other essays* published in 2006. Rudolphs are well-known and much appreciated scholars writing about India. Their book deals with Gandhi as a postmodernist. They argue that Gandhi can be termed as a postmodernist both in the *epistemological and historical sense of postmodernism.* A brief summary of their arguments is given below.

The modernist way of thinking or epistemology was challenged by Gandhi Rudolphs argue. Like postmodernists Gandhi refused to believe that there were universal truths, objective knowledge and master narratives. Gandhi was of the opinion that at best human beings can know only partial and contigent truths. His idea of truth was 'truth in action' which necessarily meant a location of truth in the facts and circumstances of the particular situation. In the spirit of science he described his pursuit of truth as 'experiment'. Gandhi compared absolute truth to a diamond which could not be seen whole but whose many facets or surfaces revealed partial truths. Like Euclid's theorem, truth was something that presented an ideal rather than a real thing. Truth, for Gandhi, could be situational as in the goal of *satyagraha,* contextual and contingent as in the experimental truths found in his autobiography, and absolute as in his commitment to 'Truth is God'.

Rudolphs hold that Gandhi is postmodern even in his hermeneutic (that is in relation to the meaning) of written texts. With regard to his acceptance of vegetarianism he sources his acceptance finally on the arguments provided by Henry Salt in his book *Plea for Vegetarianism.* He neither accepts the modernist idea of usefulness of meat nor the traditional idea of its avoidance on religious grounds. He views the *Bhagawadgita* as a poem to be read by all – something new in India where only the *upper caste men* were supposed to read it—and characterised it as a great poem where meanings of words change or expand and this is what we should learn from it. The *Gita* also does not encourage finality. What may be permissible at one time or place may not be so at another. This, according to Rudolphs, is a clinching evidence of the postmodernist makeup of Gandhi's mind. Gandhi also said that the *Gita* should not be treated as a historical work but read as a metaphor. With regard to the discussion on incarnation Gandhi argues that the message is not to show Krishna as perfect incarnation but a guide on the path of self realization.

After discussing Gandhi's epistemology to be in consonance with postmodernism the Rudoplhs try locating him in the postmodernist historical space. While Gandhi's contemporaries were lured by the gifts of modernization like progress, rationality and mechanization, Gandhi was free from all these allurements. Rather he was critical of the very aspects of modern civilization feted by others. This was amply demonstrated in *Hind Swaraj* wherein he denounced the so-called gifts of modernity. The Rudolphs consider Gandhi's critique of modern civilization in *Hind Swaraj* as 'an opening salvo of the postmodern era'. They further write that through this book 'he helped to inaugurate the postmodern era by critiquing and rejecting 'modern civilization' and by articulating a civilizational alternative to it.'[4] Rudolphs have placed Gandhi vis-à-vis Nehru on the issue of the right path of development. Gandhi challenged the modern view of "progress" which was thought to be always benign. Gandhi was vindicated when the same progress led to the Holocaust, World Wars and large scale devastation.

Rudolphs state how in the 1960s postmodern thinkers began to ask whether modernity should continue to be accepted as *the* master narrative of the era. The destruction of environment in the name of progress was brought out graphically by the publication of Rachel Carson's book *Silent Spring*.[5] War as a means of bringing about better world was disputed in the anti-Vietnam war demonstration throughout USA. Against this background, the Rudolphs write, 'Gandhi's

1909 challenge and alternative to modern civilization began to resonate with wider circles of thought and opinion. In 1909 *raj* censors had declared Gandhi's challenge to modern civilization in *Hind Swaraj* politically subversive but they didn't even notice its cultural subversions.'[6] They believe *Hind Swaraj* to be the 'text of our times".

Jyotirmaya Sharma, while reviewing Rudolphs' book for *The Hindu,* does not agree with Gandhi's characterization as a postmodernist. First, he argues with the idea of postmodernism being desirable, and, then he questions the basis on which the Rudolphs describe Gandhi as a postmodernist. Sharma has problem with the idea of self as propounded by the postmodernists vis-à-vis Gandhi's idea of self. He states: 'Gandhi's idea of the self was based on self-knowledge, and was far removed from the postmodernist idea of a self that is centreless, and constituted of `random assemblages of contingent and idiosyncratic needs...' Unlike the postmodernists, the Mahatma did entertain the idea of a `true self'. His politics flowed from this source. Equally dangerous is to construct Gandhi's model of India's villages as a polar opposite of Nehruvian high modernism, Sharma argues. In doing so, the Mahatma is uncomfortably pushed into the same slot as the Hindu nationalists, who have also approvingly endorsed Gandhi's advocacy of villages, panchayats, trusteeship and swadeshi, without a thought being expended on Gandhi's reception to the idea of a nation, which is radically different from theirs.' [7]

The debate whether Gandhi is a postmodernist or not, is still on.

REFERENCES

1. D. Hardiman, 'An alternative modernity', ***Gandhi: In His Times and Ours, 2003.*** This is the first book of the series THE INDIAN CENTURY edited by Ramachandra Guha and Sunil Khilnani. In the foreword to the book the editors state that the series would contain compelling subjects on modern Indian history. They thought it appropriate to begin their series with Gandhi. David Hardiman seems to be eminently suited for the job because of his specialization on modern Indian history and also because of his research in various peoples' movements in

Gujarat. Apart from his own interest in Gandhi, Hardiman's research and experience in Gujarat has helped him see and explain the connection between the relevance of Gandhi in his times and in present times.

2. See Appendix-II
3. *The Virtue of Non-Violence: from Gautama to Gandhi* (SUNY Press, 2004)
4. *Ibid.*, p. 3.
5. Rachel Carson was an .American marine biologist and nature writer. In 1962 she published the book *Silent Spring* bringing attention to the fact how the use of pesticides had killed bird life in USA and thus led to a season of spring devoid of the chirping sound of birds. This book was a landmark in bringing about global awareness on environmental issues.
6. Rudolphs, *op.cit.*, p. 15.
7. *The Hindu*, July 4,2006. Those desirous of reading a more technical and philosophical critique of Gandhi's Postmodernism are advised to read the excellent article by Upasana Pandey, 'Problem with Postmodern Gandhi', *Mainstream*, Vol XLV., No. 41.

PART–IV
CONCEPTS AND MOVEMENTS

There are many causes that
I am prepared to die
for but no cause
that
I am prepared to kill for.

—M.K. Gandhi

9
Nationalism

Why so jubilant? Purna swaraj *is far off.*

Have we got swaraj? Did swaraj mean only that the British rule should end? To my mind it was not so. For me Sabarmati is far off, Noakhali is near.

Mahatma Gandhi in a letter to Hariprasad Desai, an old associate who had asked Gandhi to return to Ahmedabad ashram as he had pledged on the eve of the Dandi March to go back to Sabarmati Ashram only after India attained swaraj. CWMG, Vol. LXXXVIII, p. 418.

Gandhi is an important figure in India's national movement. A phase of our national movement is called the 'Gandhian phase'. Indian children are taught from childhood that Gandhi gave Indians freedom from the British rule. All these inputs create in the Indian mind the picture of Gandhi as a great nationalist. The fact of the matter, however, is that Gandhi's ideas on nationalism were very complex and need a careful examination.

What is a nation? In broad terms a nation is defined as a people living in a definite territory for a long period of time, sharing a common language, history and culture and having a sense of belonging to that particular area. The idea of nationalism is derived from this very idea when people follow an exclusivist ideology to promote the perceived welfare of their nation— sometimes even at the expense of other nations or the world community at large. Nationalism is also equated with patriotism at times and a good deal of folklore is built around it. In short nationalism is an ideology or a psychological idea for rallying support of a people.

If nation and nationalism are defined in the narrow terms of allegiance to a particular community or country Gandhi's views do not fit into this idea of nation. Gandhi's idea of nation and nationalism was broad, democratic and moral.

Gandhi's idea of nation and nationalism were fashioned in the wake of his personal experiences and evolved along with him. Early in his life, like the nationalists of the first decade of the twentieth century- the Moderates, Gandhi had great faith in the fairness of the British Empire. His personal experiences, later, however, led him to change his mind. In 1892 when he went to see a British officer in Rajkot in connection with some work regarding his brother, Gandhi was asked to leave most unceremoniously. This was a shock for Gandhi who expected to be treated with respect by the Englishman on account of his being a trained barrister. Later while being treated in South Africa as a "coolie barrister", not being allowed to travel in first class in a train with Europeans in spite of possessing a first class ticket; and being thrown out of the compartment for refusing to shift to a third class compartment, and similar humiliating experiences made it clear to him that he was being treated thus because India was not free. *Freedom from foreign rule thus became a component of his idea of nationalism.* He organized a non -violent movement against this injustice against the government in South Africa demanding to be treated at par with other subjects of the British Empire. His faith in the British sense of justice still remained intact.

His views on the fairness of the British rulers underwent dramatic change when while helping the British in their fight against the Zulus in South Africa (1906) he encountered the worst form of racism against the Zulus practised by the British. He realized that the war against the Zulus was not a war but a manhunt where the Zulus were being killed because they dared to question the British right to tax them. This according to Hardiman, cured him of all the 'delusions about British imperialism'.[1] *His abhorrence for violent nature of the state and particularly the racist aspect of imperialism,* was consolidated at this stage. This too became an integral part of his idea of nationalism. His opposition to the British rule as a colonial oppressor began after this experience.

Gandhi discussed the idea of nationalism for the first time at great length in his booklet *Hind Swaraj* written in 1909. **He however seldom used the term nation. He preferred to use the terms *swaraj, swadesh* or Indian civilization.** By such usage he wanted to drive home the fact that his concept of nation was very different from the western notion of nation, which was at times 'collectivist, monolithic, aggressive and xenophobic'(Haridman). The Italian, German, French and British concept of nationality suffered from all these weaknesses. Gandhian view of the Indian nation was a spiritual, non-violent, inclusive and peaceful nation.

In *Hind Swaraj* Gandhi discusses at length the idea of Indian nation. *National independence* was an important stage of Indian nationalism, he concedes. But when asked whether India should follow the Italian example and throw out the British from India by violent means Gandhi gives a clear 'no' for an answer. His argument is that since violence is irrevocable hence it should be used after utmost consideration. Man being fallible, should not use it against anyone. Making a case against the use of violence he further clarified that anything that was won through violence has to be maintained through violence which is not the essence of Indian civilization. He does not support the Italian method of winning independence or the Italian concept of nationalism as it means freedom for only the upper classes of society.

Gandhi was of the firm opinion that despite its multifarious castes, religions and cultures India has always been a nation though the west never recognized it as such. Here, in response to an observation by the 'reader' that because of its disunity, Indians can hardly qualify themselves to be called a nation Gandhi states, 'The English have taught us that we were not one nation before and that it will require centuries before we become one nation. This is without foundation. We were one nation before they came to India. One thought inspires us. Our mode of life was the same. It was because we were one nation that they were able to establish one kingdom. Subsequently they divided us.'[2] Nationalism for India is not new, he asserted, as the four *mathas* (spiritual abodes, seats) in four corners of India prove.[3] Gandhi further goes on to say that *nationalism in not a foreign construct*, it is very much an Indian idea practiced even before the Europeans became aware of it. Had India not been a nation the British would not have referred to their acquisitions in this subcontinent as 'India', Gandhi argues.

Gandhi is clear that a *nation need not be co-terminus with religion*. Alluding to the discourse of the times, when the 'reader' persists and states that India may have been a nation when it was a homogeneous country in terms of religion and that ever since the Muslims or Christians came to India this homogeneity was destroyed hence India could no longer qualify to be a nation, Gandhi emphatically counters this view. Gandhi declares that all those who are born in India or live in India are Indians and they belong to the Indian nation. About the Hindu- Muslim question he further clarifies that the issue of differences have been exaggerated to some extent by the British Government for its selfish purpose. Indians have also contributed to this impression by their constant bickering. If the brothers have good understanding no outsider can sow seeds of division, Gandhi opined.

In *Hind Swaraj* Gandhi expounded the *broad view of Indian nation. It was a civilization with deep moral and spiritual grounding* that ruled out hatred for even the rulers, that is, the British. They were welcome to continue staying in India provided they took to Indian civilization. The Indian civilization was also not chauvinistic but based on human rights, women's assertion, democratic governance, respect for all races, castes and religions and the use of least amount of force.

Gandhi believed that India, as a vast federation of village republics, could join the great family of nation states as an equal partner. *The Gujarati text of Hind Swaraj, as Anthony J. Parel has pointed out, makes a significant difference between a genuine nation formed as community (praja) and a nation of individuals merely held together by state power (rashtra).* As opposed to the popular view that it was British administration and British railways that made India a nation, Gandhi claimed that 'India has been one country right from ancient times.' Pilgrim saints, who walked the length and breadth of the Indian subcontinent, unified India centuries before it was linked by iron rails. Today millions of Indians still ply these British-built railways, not only to do business and visit relatives, but to continue the age old pilgrimage to the sacred sites of Mother India. Later in his other writings Gandhi continued reflecting on the idea of nation and nationalism and expounding it further.

Writing for his newspaper, *Young India*, Gandhi elaborated upon as to how his idea of nationalism encompassed the whole of the human race through the concept of the principle of *hierarchy of allegiances*—for family, self was to be sacrificed; for village, family; for state, village; for nation , state; and, for humanity, nation was to be sacrificed. Gandhi wrote on March 3, 1925.

> Just as the cult of patriotism teaches us today that the individual has to die for the family, the family has to die for the village, the village for the district, the district for the province, and the province for the country, even so a country has to be free that it may die, if necessary, for the benefit of the world. My love, therefore, of nationalism is that my country may become free, that if need be the whole of the country may die, so that the human race my live.

Therefore *service to humanity was the highest goal to be*

achieved in Gandhi's concept of nationality. His concept of nationalism did not rule out people of different races or countries. In other words his nation reflects the idea of the ancient Indian concept of *vasudhaiva kutumbakam*—the world is our family. Gandhi fought for the independence of the country because he believed that only an independent India could be of service to the world.

As a corollary to the above conception of the world being one, *Gandhi's nationalism seeks not to harm any nation* but believes in presenting before the warring countries of the world through its example a novel method of settling mutual disputes through dialogues and nonviolence. He wrote:

> My patriotism is not an exclusive thing. It is all-embracing and I should reject that patriotism which sought to mount upon the distress or exploitation of other nationalities. The conception of my patriotism is nothing if it is not always, in every case without exception , consistent with the broadest good of humanity at large. (*Young India*, 4.4.29)

It is no wonder, therefore, that Gandhi was deeply moved when the German planes bombarded the city of London though he was at the time contemplating the Quit India movement asking the British government to leave India to its fate.

Gandhi's innate spiritual approach to life made him view the concept of nation also in spiritual terms. The Indian *nation of his conception was basically individual spirituality writ large*—that is, a collection of spiritually enlightened people. *Swaraj* was the guiding principle. A people in full control of their senses form the collectivity called the independent nation. Thus truth and non-violence are practiced not only in personal dealings but also in public affairs. Rights flow from duties well observed. In other words, no external restrictions on liberties are required since people regulate their behaviour on the basis of truth and non-violence.

Gandhi's concept of nation is *based on democratic principle* but democratic governance is not to be guided by majoritarianism. It takes care of the views of all sections of the public. The *society is also formed along democratic lines.* The state does not discriminate between the rich and the poor, the agriculturist and the industrialist, the village and the town. Caste and religion do not come in the way of communal living and people of different faiths live in harmony with each other. The basic amenities of life, which only the rich enjoyed so far, are made available to all. Gandhi's nationalism was what Hardiman describes as 'incorporative nationalism' It does not exclude any sect, race, class or caste. In this respect, Gandhi's idea of nation is much different from the concept of *rashtra* or nation propounded by VD Savarkar or Jinnah..[4]

Gandhi's unusual views on nation and nationalism were misunderstood during his lifetime both by the international community and his closest friends. This was so because he was active as a leader in the fight for India's freedom from the British rule. Gandhi saw no contradiction in fighting against the British and extolling the virtues of the English people. Freedom for India was a precondition for reaching the goal of serving humanity irrespective of international boundaries because he firmly believed that an independent India would have much to teach to the world whereas an India in chains had nothing to offer to its people or the world at large. The methods adopted by Gandhi during the non-cooperation movement in 1920-22 calling for boycott of British goods and burning of British cloth were considered negative and narrow-minded steps by Rabindranath Tagore who was otherwise an admirer of Gandhi. Similarly, CF Andrews, popularly known as Deenbandhu, found the burning of foreign cloth reflecting racist feelings.[5] Gandhi reported both these objections prominently in his newspapers with justification for his moves. To Tagore's objection he clarified that India's freedom was a prerequisite to internationalism and therefore his non-cooperation movement was not negative. One has to negate untruth in order to arrive at truth.[6] Gandhi's slogan asking British to quit India was also objected to by some of his longstanding British friends as being anti- British. In this regard even so many years after India's independence Gandhi is misunderstood or deliberately misinterpreted by our politicians. When the issue of Mrs Sonia Gandhi's foreign origin was raked up by political parties as a disqualification for fighting elections or against Indian self respect, the leader of AIADMK party, J. Jayalalitha famously commented that Gandhi led the Indians in a fight asking the whites to quit India and now we are inviting a white woman to become our Prime Minister! Gandhi had clarified during the discussion on this topic that he is not against the English staying in India. He only wanted the British *government* to leave India and let Indians govern themselves.

It is also interesting to know that Gandhi was nominated for the Nobel Peace Prize thrice in his lifetime in 1937, in 1938 and in 1939.When he was nominated the first time in 1937, the advisor to the Nobel Committee, Professor Jacob Worm-Muller objected to his getting the prize because in his opinion, Gandhi was a nationalist as 'his fight was for Indians only' in South Africa and not for blacks whose condition was worse, and, as such, Gandhi was 'too much of an Indian nationalist'. In later years his nomination was rejected on the grounds that he was an inconsistent pacifist as he had campaigned for enlisting soldiers for the British during WWI. He was also accused of not being farsighted enough to see that his popular movements could generate into violent struggles. In the last year of his life he was accused of hinting at the appropriateness of war in 1947 when Pakistan attacked India. The last reason was dropped after his death when he was once again considered for the Nobel Peace Prize—for the fourth time. This could not be given as there was no heir to Gandhi and hence the committee did not award Nobel Peace prize to any one that year.[7]

To sum up one can say that Gandhi was not a nationalist in the conventional sense of the term. He believed in inclusive rather than exclusive nationalism. For him love for one's own country does not mean that one should think evil of another country and its people or, by actions, seek to harm other countries or people. For him nationalism should respect humanism otherwise it is of a vulgar order. The ultimate aim of his nationalism was internationalism which in other words, was service to humanity. For practising internationalism, a country must be free from foreign rule, must have democratic government, be a society free from discriminations based on caste, creed, sex, race and region, have an equitable economic system and be based on moral and spiritual values. For such a society outside regulation or force would be unnecessary since the citizen would self regulate their actions.

His nationalism was open to influences from outside while being firmly grounded in the spiritual values of India. He had famously remarked:

> I do not want my house to be walled in on all sides and my windows to be stuffed. I want the cultures of all the lands to be blown about my house as freely as possible. But I refuse to be blown off my feet by any. I refuse to live in other people's houses as an interloper, a beggar or a slave.[8]

Gandhi's views on nationhood are not modernist. As Parel states: '[*Hind Swaraj*] does not propound the *modern* concept of nation in so far as the latter is based on the notions of brute force, the priority of national interest, and a principle of exclusiveness based either religion, or language, or race.' Even the relatively innocuous state apparatus of liberal democracy does not escape Gandhi's critical eye. Although it is theoretically designed to do so, liberal democracies do not empower individuals; rather, as Parekh so aptly phrases it, they abstract 'power from the people, concentrate it in the state and then return it to them in their new [abstract roles] as citizens.'

On the basis of the views of Anthony Parel and Bhikhu Parekh on Gandhi's political philosophy some scholars have concluded that Gandhi's notion of nation is post modernist because it is based on decentralized local control and assimilation and toleration of cultural differences. This argument has been further developed by the Rudolphs in their book *Postmodern Gandhi* published in 2006.

In a recent study[9] Anthony J Parel has given a new name to Gandhi's idea of nationalism—'civic nationalism'. Emphasizing the harmonizing nature of Gandhian thought Parel is of the view that Gandhi's writings can be better appreciated if we study them in the intellectual context of the theory of *purushartha* found in Hindu philosophy because that is how Gandhi viewed nationalism. The *purusharthas* or strivings of life are four- *kama, artha, dharma* and *moksha.* Under *artha* Parel discusses the Gandhi's views on civic nationalism, the state and economy. Parel states that Gandhi rejected the religion based nationalism of the Muslim League and the ethnic nationalism of Savarkar. He promoted the idea of civic nationalism based on the idea of an Indian being a citizen of a territorial entity with full opportunity for self-growth and social development despite multiple identities. Religion, caste, class or gender of a person was irrelevant in so far as the enjoyment of rights was concerned. As the inhabitant of the territory he was entitled to rights since his birth, with the constitution merely recognizing them.

To conclude one may say that Gandhi's concept of nationalism was unique and had strong ethical and moral underpinnings.

REFERENCES

1. David Hardiman,*Gandhi in His Times and Ours,* Permanent Black, 2003, p. 1.
2. *Hind Swaraj,* p. 40.
3. *Ibid.,* The four *mathas* Gandhi is referring to are Badrinath in the north, Shringeri in the south, Puri in the east and Dwarka in the west.
4. Gandhi's idea of nationalism was diametrically opposed to the idea of nationalism held by Veer Savarkar or Mohammad Ali Jinnah. According to Savarkar only who considered India as their pitribhumi and punyabhumi belonged to the rashtra. By this definition, the Muslims satisfied only one condition— that of *pitribhumi* since their *punyabhumi* was in Saudi Arabia where their supreme religious allegiance lay. Therefore, according to Savarkar they did not consitute the *Hindu rashtra.* They could become an integral part of the *rashtra* only if they gave up links with Saudi Arabia where they go for *haj.* Similarly,

Jinnah considered Hindus and Muslims as belonging to separate nations since, according to him, their religion, language and culture differed. Hence he clamoured for a separate country for Muslims where they could form majority government and be ruled by Muslims alone. Gandhi countered Savarkar's idea of nation by stating that Hindus and Muslims were the children of India who drew sustenance from mother India and therefore religious differences did not matter. With Jinnah he argued that since in matters of public policy religion had no role to play therefore whether one belonged to one religion or other did not affect governance or enjoyment of public amenities.

5. 'Ethics of Destruction', *Young India, Collected Works of Mahatma Gandhi (CWMG)*, Vol.XXi .1.9.21, p. 41.
6. See Appendix -IV of *CWMG*, Vol.XX
7. Øyvind Tønnesson, 'Mahatma Gandhi, the Missing Laureate,' Nobel e-Museum Peace Editor, 1998-2000, December 1, 1999.
8. *Harijan*, 7-7-1946, p. 212.
9. Anthony J Parel, *Gandhi's Philosophy and Quest for Harmony*,. Cambridge, Cambridge University Press, 2006.

10
Gandhi's Views on Communal Unity

A civilization is to be judged by the treatment of its minorities.

—MK Gandhi

Gandhi was one of the greatest champions of communal unity in India. He lived his whole life striving for it, ensuring it, and finally attained martyrdom at the altar of communal harmony.

Childhood Experiences: Gandhi's views on communal unity were largely influenced by his family background and upbringing. Gandhi's father, Karamchand Gandhi, was a *Vallabhacharya Vaishnav,* a community generally very strict about inter-dining with other communities, but being the *diwan* of Rajkot he had to interact with people of different faiths. Gandhi was, however, more influenced by his mother, the fourth wife of his father, and being the youngest in the family, he was very close to her. Gandhi had three siblings—two brothers, Laxmidas and Karsandas, and one sister, Raliatbehn. His mother, Putlibai, belonged to *Parnami* sect which was founded in the early 18th century by Prannath who preached that the Puranas, the Koran and the Bible represented merely alternative paths to One God. No images were allowed in Parnami temples where scriptures of different religions were placed. Apart from his mother's influence, being a precocious and sensitive child, Gandhi was deeply moved by the stories of Raja Harischandra who sacrificed his all for truth, and the story of Shravan Kumar who was a devoted son. Thus, Gandhi grew up in an environment of composite culture, representing different religions except Christianity, which did not have much favour with the upper sections of the community because of the activities of some of the missionaries in converting tribals to their faith, particularly in the Saurashtra region. The influences in these formative years were largely responsible for his religious and spiritual views later. He affirmed his childhood impressions during a speech in 1947 where he asserted that his belief in complete brotherhood among Hindus, Muslims and Parsis dated back to before 1885 when he was barely 12 years old.[1]

Experiences in London: In 1888 Gandhi left for England to study law. In England, being viewed as an Indian and a Hindu, Gandhi was expected to be conversant with the Hindu religious scriptures. He had not read any of these and therefore diligently set himself to study them. He read the *Gita*, translated as *The Celestial Song* by Edwin Arnold and also read the biography of Buddha written by the same author. He studied the Bible and books on Zoarashtrianism.. Combined with these readings, his exposure to liberal thought in Britain formed his views on the relation between religion and state.

Experiences in South Africa: Gandhi came into contact with missionaries and Christian religious literature and practices in a big way while he was in South Africa for fighting a lawsuit there. At one point of time there was a pressure on him to convert to Christianity because he was impressed by the sense of service and suffering in the Christian faith. Gandhi did not convert because he found the concept of a person being God or the idea that God revealed the true religion to a chosen person, problematic. Even in his own faith he did not believe in Rama or Krishna as historical persons. His idea of Rama was that of the supreme God and who represented the Truth. Later on he dispensed with even the name and declared that Truth itself was God.

It is interesting to recall that in South Africa Gandhi was

considered a representative of Indian community and when he was to go to England as the head of a delegation to represent the case of Indians, some Hindus in Transvaal wanted the deputation to include an additional Hindu 'to balance Ali' a Muslim member of the delegation, underlining the non-communal standing of Gandhi. The idea of multi-faith prayers that Gandhi was to follow later in life also was born in South Africa where in his settlements like the Phoenix farm, people belonging to all faiths lived.

Gandhi's Religion: Gleaning good points from different religions, Gandhi had formed his own conception of religion which did not correspond fully with any one religion. JTF Jordans therefore aptly titles his book describing Gandhi's faith as *Gandhi's Religion: A Homespun Shawl.* Gandhi believed in the 'religion which was above all religions' (*Hind Swaraj).* Compassion for all sentient beings was the hallmark of this religion. Therefore his favourite bhajan was *Vaishnava jana to tene kahiye je peed parayi jane re*—he is a true *vaishnava,* who empathizes with the suffering of others.' According to Gandhi one should not abandon compassion even if his or her religious scriptures said so. One should not follow one's religious books blindly because though all religions proceed from the same God 'all are imperfect because they have come down to us through imperfect human instrumentality.'[2]

Gandhi's Writings on Communal Unity:

Hind Swaraj:

His earliest writings on the communal question are found in his book *Hind Swaraj.* In this booklet a full chapter is devoted to it (Chapter X). As is already discussed, one of the reasons for writing *Hind Swaraj* was to address the question of violence that had crept into the freedom struggle of India. This violence was largely attributed to the provocation by the British government's act of Partitioning the province of Bengal, the centre of nationalist sentiments, along communal lines with the intention of dividing the people. The *swadeshi* movement which was launched to undo this Partition unwittingly divided the people along communal lines because some of its leaders, unmindful of the Muslims sensitivities followed practices with which Muslims were not very comfortable. Though Gandhi was in South Africa when this movement was going on in India he was aware of the developments. Against this background, Gandhi brought in the question of Indian nation with reference to Hindus and Muslims in *Hind Swaraj*.

During the discussion with the 'editor' when Gandhi says that India has been a nation even before the advent of the British rule, and cites the example of four centres of Hindu holy places, *mathas,* in four corners of India as a proof, the reader enquires whether India continued to remain a nation when Muslims came to India. The 'reader', by implication, meant that Hindus and Muslims had such irreconcilable differences that they could not be part of one nation.

Gandhi rejects the stand and states in unequivocal terms that the Hindus, Muslims, Parsis and Christians who have made India their country are fellow-countrymen and they will have to live in unity, for their own interest. He further *questioned the 'one-religion one state'* theory by stating: 'In no part of the world are one nationality and one religion synonymous terms; nor has it ever been so in India.'[3] He also takes up the issue of *cow-slaughter* that was the reason behind the animosity between the two communities sometimes even leading to killings of members of the both communities. He advised the Hindus to try to explain to their Muslim brothers the significance of cow in their religion and persuade them not to kill the animal. If the latter did not listen, Gandhi wrote 'If I were overfull of pity for the cow, I should sacrifice my life to save her but not take my brother's.'[4] He also criticized the cow-protection societies that had cropped up because these societies did not care for the cows when they are alive and allowed them to be mistreated but came into action only when Muslims slaughtered them. Lastly, he argued, if Hindus say that they believe in the principle of non-killing how come they kill a fellow man? Besides some Hindus also partake of meat and are not excluded from India because of that. The animosity between the two communities is largely the doing of the British who project Hindus and Muslims as separate nations.

Gandhi emphasizes the fact that good relations between the two communities can be built only if both make *sincere efforts to understand each other's religions.* 'Those who do not wish to misunderstand things may read up the Koran, and they will find therein hundreds of passages acceptable to the Hindus; and the Bhagwadgita contains passages to which not a Mahomedan can take exception.'[5] When the two communities do so, the British will not be able to sow dissensions. Using a commonplace imagery Gandhi further reinforces his argument: 'The way to save the pot is not to keep it away from the danger point but to bake it so that no stone would break it.'[6] He asks the Hindus to take the first step in the direction of communal unity since they are in majority. He also refers to the sense of insecurity among the Muslims which has made them ask for special concessions from Lord Morley in the form of Separate Electorate for Muslims. Therefore it is necessary that the Hindus should make all efforts to 'inspire confidence' among the Muslims.

Other Writings:

Later on in many of his writings Gandhi came back to the issue of communal harmony. This became frequent when the communal situation became volatile after the sudden suspension of the Non-Cooperation Movement in 1922.The Moplah rebellion in the south, which was basically a fight between the tillers and landlords, took a communal colour as the farmers were mainly poor Muslims whereas the landlords were Hindus. The great Hindu-Muslim unity that was seen during the Non-Cooperation Movement vanished. Gandhi and Ali Brothers, the architects of this unity, also parted ways. Fifteen to twenty riots a year became the order of the day for almost a decade following the suspension. Gandhi was constrained to write a series of articles in his newspaper *Young India* in May 1924 which were later published in the form of a pamphlet entitled *Hindu-Muslim Tension: its Cause and Cure.* This article did not help the situation. Some of the remarks made by him about Muslims, irked the community and distanced them from him. Despite his clarifications and apologies the rift continued to widen. At this point he also took up cudgels against the *Arya Samajis* who had become very active in Punjab. There was a virulent propaganda conducted between the fundamentalists among the Arya Samajis and Muslims against each other, further worsening the communal situation. In order to assuage the feelings of Hindus, Gandhi also entered into dialogue with Christian missionaries because of the tension over conversions of tribals to Christianity and some questionable missionary activities in some parts of India.

In a desperate attempt to forge the *heart unity,* which according to him was at the center of communal unity in India Gandhi wrote extensively in the columns of his newspapers *Navajivan, Harijanbandhu* (Gujarati), *Young India, Harijan* (English) and *Harijan Sewak* (Hindi) about the good points of all religions— Hinduism, Buddhism, Christianity and Islam. Gandhi could discern noble principles in all religions and asked Indians not only to show toleration and respect to faiths other than their own, instead have genuine 'goodwill' for different religions. He was of the opinion that there was a religion above all religions that was to be followed by followers of all faiths. He appreciated Hinduism for its 'tolerance' and Buddhism for giving Hinduism a 'new life and a new interpretation' by rejecting the idea that God needed animal sacrifice to be pleased and also for emphasizing and re-declaring the 'eternal and unalterable existence of the moral government of this universe'. Gandhi appreciated Islam for its uncompromising belief in the oneness of God and brotherhood of man. Though he did not believe in ascribing exclusive divinity to Jesus he appreciated and respected the principles of suffering and service in the Christian faith.

On Proselytization : Since all religions had something good to offer to humanity, Gandhi did not approve of forced conversions from one religion to another. He wanted men and women to be a good Hindu or a good Muslim or a good Christian rather than looking for redemption in a religion in which they are not born. Speaking against the *Shuddhi* movement launched by the *Arya Samajists* for reconverting people from other faith to Hinduism, or the Muslim version of *Shuddhi* movement, the *Tabligh* movement, he wrote:

> The real *Shuddhi* movement should consist in each one trying to arrive at perfection in his or her own faith. In such a plan character would be the only test. What is the use of crossing from one compartment to another, if does not mean a moral rise?[7]

As referred to earlier, he also entered into dialogue with Christian missionaries because of the tension over conversion of tribals to Christianity and some questionable missionary activities in some parts of India.

Gandhi's Actions for Communal Unity:

Gandhi was a man of action. Not only did he believe in and write on communal unity but practised it in real life as well. He encouraged his associates and people in general to do the same. To bring about a 'heart unity' was one of the projects of his Constructive Programme. The inmates of the ashrams that he established in South Africa and India were under pledge to promote and practise communal unity. The members of the Congress Party were expected to be respectful to all religions.

Communal riots grieved him no end. He put his physical safety and life at stake for ensuring communal harmony. At the height of communal tension in Noakhali (1946) he went alone to douse the communal fires. His prayer meetings were many a time disturbed by fanatics but he carried on without caring for his life. He refused to take bodyguards when threatened by such communal groups. An attack on his life was made even before[8] he was finally assassinated by Nathu Ram Godse, yet he was totally fearless.

REFERENCES

1. *CWMG* Vol. XCVI, p. 330.
2. *Young India,* 29-5-24.
3. MK Gandhi, *Hind Swaraj,* p. 43.
4. *ibid.,* p. 44.
5. *ibid.,* p. 46.
6. *ibid.*
7. *Young India,* 29.5.24.
8. On 20th January, 1948 a bomb was thrown at one of his prayer meetings and Gandhi narrowly escaped death.

11
Gandhi on Untouchability

It has always been a mystery to me how men feel themselves honoured by the humiliation of their fellow beings.

—Mahatma Gandhi

Gandhi was the first Indian leader to make the removal of untouchability a national issue and give it as much importance as the freedom of the country from foreign rule.

Gandhi's concept of *swaraj* envisaged a society based on equality irrespective of caste, class, religion, sex or place of birth. The very idea of a section of people being treated as 'untouchable', 'un-seeable' or 'unapproachable' was, therefore, against the grain of *swaraj*. As Gandhi mentioned in his *Autobiography* and later in several of his speeches, ever since his childhood days he found the practice of untouchability repugnant to his sense of justice. He was able to empathize with the untouchables more closely after his experiences in South Africa where every Indian—rich or poor, educated or uneducated—was treated as an untouchable only because of the colour of his/her skin.

Gandhi's innate sense of justice revolted against the ill-treatment meted out to people branded as untouchables. He was determined to remove the practice of untouchability as he considered it a blot on Hinduism. Removal of untouchability had always been a recurring theme in all the movements he launched in India and South Africa. It was one of the main programs of the Non-Cooperation Movement along with the propagation of *khadi* and stress on communal unity.

What is untouchability:

Untouchability is a practice peculiar to India where a section of people are considered as untouchables because of the caste in which they are born. Such castes are considered the lowest in the ladder of social life and the castes superior to them do not inter-marry, inter -dine or allow them to share public amenities with them. Traditionally such castes were assigned lowly work as scavenging, removal of hides from dead animals, rituals associated with dead and similar such activities that were considered unclean by others and because they were engaged in such activities, they were branded as 'impure' or 'unclean' and, therefore, 'untouchables'. Even when these communities did not engage in the so-called 'unclean' work they were considered 'untouchables' by virtue of their caste. The *chandalas* and *doms* who handled dead human beings and animals, the *chamars* who were cobblers, the toddy tappers , the *bhangis* engaged in scavenging were considered as untouchables even if they did not engage in such professions. Similarly in the south the *sudras, atisudras,* the *antyajas,* the *ahandalas,* the *panchamas* and the *avarnas* come in this category. Gandhi waged an all-out war against this practice.

Gandhi's Approach:

Gandhi's approach towards the problem was not confrontationist. He approached the so called upper castes that practised untouchability and argued with them that the system had no sanction in religion, and even if it were sanctioned by religion, because of its inhuman character, it need not be followed and that they should do penance for practising such an inhuman thing against their brethren over all these centuries. This approach was not liked by Dalit leaders like Ambedkar who found it too patronizing. Llyod Rudolph, a scholar on Gandhi, during a lecture addressed to students of Delhi University on 15th February 2007, however appreciated Gandhi's stand and said that this approach has been followed in USA to tackle the race problem and has been very successful.

Gandhi's Changing Views on the Relationship between Varnas, Caste and the Problem of Untouchability

Gandhi was steadfast in his belief that untouchablity was a crime against humanity and had to go. Gandhi had, however, different views regarding the relationship of untouchability with the caste system in different phases of his life. Earlier he was of the view that caste system was the modern version of the *varnashram* system according to which the Hindu society was divided into four *varnas* on the basis of the occupation pursued by each *varna*. The Brahmins were supposed to pursue learning, the Kshatriyas' duty was to defend the country and maintain law and order, the Vaishyas engaged in trade and commerce, the Sudras were supposed to work as farmers and artisans. This division, Gandhi believed, was based on the natural inclination of the person concerned and was not inflexible. One could move from one *varna* to another without any problem. Also, there was no hierarchy among these *varnas*. He believed that the present caste system has become corrupted to some extent and therefore should go back to the old system based on division of labour rather than following any system of hierarchy of castes. This view about the caste system was flawed and Dr. Ambedkar rightly pointed this out to him.

The caste system was also responsible for the inhuman system of treating a section of society as 'untouchables' who were below even the Sudras in the *varna* or caste (*jati*) hierarchy. They were the 'Atisudras'. Over a period of time and after being exposed to Dr. Ambedkar's stand Gandhi realized that he was in the wrong about defending the caste system and treating the question of untouchability separate from the evils of the caste system. In the last phase of his life Gandhi resolved to bless only those marriages that were solemnized between the so-called upper caste and untouchables.

Movement for the eradication of untouchability:

Gandhi was to a large extent instrumental in bringing the issue of untouchability on to the center-stage of the Indian national movement by extensive writing on the subject supplemented by tours and personal contact programmes. Never before had untouchability in India been exposed to such a systematic, organized and large scale attack. Commenting on it, Pt Nehru had observed:

> In our own period numerous movements to break the tyranny of the caste have risen among the middle classes and they have made a difference, but not a vital one, so far as masses are concerned. Their movement was usually of direct attack. Then Gandhi came and tackled the problem after the immemorial Indian fashion, in an indirect way, and his eyes were on the masses. He had been direct enough, aggressive enough, persistent enough, but without challenging the original basic functional theory underlying the four main castes. He has attacked the rank undergrowth and over growth, knowing well that he was undermining the whole caste structure thereby.[1]

From 1930 onwards eradication of untouchability became a mission with Gandhi. His confrontation with Dr Ambedkar at the Second Round Table Conference in London in 1931 made him see through the British game of dividing the nation once again by projecting Dr. Ambedkar as the sole representative of the Depressed Classes[2] and agreeing to award separate electorate to the Depressed Classes. This made him aware of the urgency to address the issue. Therefore, at the Conference itself he declared that he would put his life at stake and oppose the award of separated electorate to the Depressed Classes as contemplated by the British. When the British declared the Ramsay McDonald Award in 1932 in which Separate Electorate was provided for the Depressed Classes, Gandhi, then in jail, went on fast unto death for the withdrawal of the Award. As his condition deteriorated, efforts were made to come to some kind of compromise between Ambedkar's stand and Gandhi's stand. Finally, the compromise was reached in the Poona Pact whereby Gandhi agreed to reservation of seats for the Depressed Classes as a lesser evil. At this point Gandhi also requested the British government to permit him to give press statements against untouchability from jail and continue to work for the abolition of untouchability from the jail itself.

Gandhi issued 13 'Statements on Untouchability' from prison (November 4, 1932 to December 30, 1932) that touched upon various issues related to the practice. He pointed out the religion does not authorize untouchability. To prove his point he sent a questionnaire consisting of ten questions, to Sanskrit scholars asking them to give him references from Hindu scriptures that justified untouchability. On receipt of a reply that untouchability as practiced in the present times does not have any reference in the scriptures Gandhi published a public statement signed by the learned scholars. Adding that even if the scriptures justified untouchability he would not have accepted it as it was against humanity.

Some *Sanatanists* argued with Gandhi that the untouchables are reaping the fruits of the past karma by being born as untouchables and therefore humans had no right to interfere in God's dispensation. Gandhi said that if that was so they have already had enough punishment and society should not compound their misery further.

His strategy for tackling the evil of untouchability was as follows:

1. On the suggestion of a reader he chose to describe the untouchables as Harijans that 'is the children of god' so as to do away with the term 'untouchable.'[3] Gandhi however made it clear:

   The term has not been coined with a view to perpetuating the separate identity of Harijans...The term untouchable savours of contempt...as untouchables have a distinct identity we must have a name by which to call them...Let us pray that this separateness may be done away with so that all of us may become fit to be called 'Harijans' –men of God. A friend rightly said that today caste Hindus have become 'Arijans'–enemies of Hinduism.[4]
2. Gandhi tried to spread awareness against the evils of

untouchability by actively involving the so-called upper castes in order to change their mindset. This he did by starting three newspapers which became his 'views papers' – *Harijan* in English, *Harijan Sewak* in Hindi and *Harijanbandhu* in Gujarati.

3. He established the *Harijan Sewak Sangh* devoted to the uplift of Harijans.
4. He conducted 'Harijan tours' throughout the length and breadth of India spreading his message against untouchability.
5. Gandhi also supported the movement for throwing open temples for Harijans. However, he did not adopt a confrontationist policy in the matter. He made it a point that unless the majority of the temple-goers gave their assent to the opening of temples to Harijans he would not press for it. In case of a prestigious temple in South India, he went a step further and organized referendum to know the wishes of the temple-goers and silence the critics who spread the rumours that Gandhi was going against the wishes of the high caste people.
6. The Vaikom Satyagraha in Kerala which was organized for allowing the use of road near temple for untouchables also was supported by Gandhi initially though later it was taken up by the local leaders who succeeded in their attempt.
7. Gandhi was not averse to taking the help of law if it helped reformers. Inspired by intensive propaganda taking place against untouchability some enlightened legislators with reformist bent of mind introduced Bills aimed at removing the disabilities placed on Harijans by some Provincial Governments and in some provisions of law, from entering temples. In the 1930s two Bills were awaiting Viceroy's sanction, one for introduction in the Central Legislative Assembly by Ranga Iyer and the other for introduction in Madras Council by Subbaroyan. Gandhi gave wide publicity to these Bills and implored legislators to give their full support to them. Later, after his death when the

Constituent Assembly of India included Article 17 in the Constitution declaring the abolition of untouchability the Assembly resounded with cries of "Mahatma Gandhi ki Jai".

8. Gandhi entered into dialogue with other reform movements for the untouchables like the movement led by Narayan Guru in Kerala and the Self Respect Movement led by E.V. Ramaswamy. He, however, did not form a common front with them.

Gandhi's views regarding untouchability were not appreciated by Hindu *sanatanists* who thought he was interfering in their religion, propagating defiance to the scriptures and coming in the way of God's method of dealing with men and women. The Muslims did not appreciate his being confined to a communal issue and asked him to devote his energies to the issue of step-motherly treatment meted out to the minority communities by the majority community and for all practical purposes treating them also as untouchables. The political leadership considered it a digression on the part of Gandhi who they believed should have been pooling in all his resources towards achieving independence from British rule rather than focusing on a social problem that could be taken care of after India became independent. Some untouchable leaders like Ambedkar found Gandhi's approach patronizing and too soft and did not have faith in its efficacy. They wanted him to take on a confrontationist approach rather than a compromising one. In spite of these criticisms and objections Gandhi carried on his movement undeterred.

To sum up one can say that Gandhi was instrumental in giving a new name 'Harijan' that is, the children of God to the so called untouchables. The Constitution of independent India classified them as Scheduled Castes and provided for universal adult franchise and equal rights for them with other castes along with reservation of seats in panchayats, and legislatures at State and National level. Seats are also reserved for them in educational institutions and government jobs. These provisions have made some difference but the social and economic status of the Dalits leaves much to be desired. Most of them are still poor, illiterate and jobless. They are still at the receiving end of discrimination by the so called upper castes especially in rural areas. In the 1970s the Dalit movement became violent under the Dalit Panthers. Under Kashi Ram and Mayawati the Dalits aquired a new name 'Bahujans' ie., 'those in majority' and made their impact felt through electoral politics. In the whole process, however, the movement has become a movement of assertion of caste identity rather than uplift. It is also not homogeneous. Regional castes dominate it and promote their vested interests. The poorest of poor of Gandhi's conception still remain unattended.

A heartening development in the empowerment of Dalits was witnessed recently when Mayawati won majority in the UP Assembly elections in 2007 and formed her government. She also modified her earlier stand of confrontation with the Brahmins and co-opted them as her allies. Some have called this as social engineering that bodes well for Indian democracy. Yet Gandhi's dream of total eradication of untouchability remains unfulfilled.

REFERENCES

1. Jawaharlal Nehru, *The Discovery of India,* New Delhi, 1960, p. 110.
2. The term 'Depressed Classes' was used in the early thirties to denote the untouchables and was in use during the period of petitions The term ' Dalit' is a self given term of recent origin. Baburao Bagul include among Dalits, adivasis, toiling classes and women. Ghanshyam Shah expanded the term to include converted untouchable Muslims. Ambedkar used it infrequently (Marathi word).

   The 1935 Act used the term Scheduled Castes to denote the Dalits. Being a purely legal term it did not have any emotional content. According to some dalit writers the term 'Harijan' denoted a passive identity and they are of the opinion that harijan uplift was used by Congress both for patronage and vote bank.

   It is interesting to note that the category of Dalit was used by no less a person than Dr Ambedkar in his fortnightly called *Bahishkrut Bharat.* It was not a mere linguistic expression, but was defined by him in a most comprehensive way. He wrote: "...dalithood is a kind of life conditions which characterize the exploitation, suppression and marginalization of Dalits by the social, economic, cultural and political domination of the upper castes' Brahminical ideology"(Kasbe 1985; Omvedt 1994). Ambedkar, however, did not use this category very often in his writings. In fact, he used a number of categories depending on the context. Eg., if he was dealing with the imperial, he would use the category of Depressed Classes, for that was permissible within the imperial official setting(Government of Maharashtra,1991:216). If he was addressing high caste Hindu adversaries, he would use the term *Bahishkrut* meaning one who is an outcast. In the arena of competitive politics, he would use the term Scheduled Caste. This was evident when he established Scheduled Caste Federation in 1952. Finally when addressing his own social constituency, he preferred to use the term 'Pad Dalit', meaning those who are crushed under the Hindu system.

In recent years some politicians have also discarded the Dalit category as socially reactionary, negative one and sought to replace it with Bahujan category (Bagul, 1981).

3. Gandhi is criticized by some for adopting a patronizing attitude towards the so-called untouchables by giving them the name of 'Harijans'. The word was not coined by Gandhi. It was proposed in 1931 by an 'untouchable' reader of *Navajivan,* who referred to its use by the Gujarati saint poet, Narsi Mehta, the author of Gandhi's favourite bhajan, 'Vaishnava Jana.'
4. *Harijan Sewak,* 28 April, 1933,*CWMG,* Vol. 61. p. 16.

12
Gandhi on Women's Question

I have mentally become a woman in order to steal into her heart.

–M.K. Gandhi

An assessment of Gandhi on women's question is a difficult task. At one level Gandhi appears to be influenced by his patriarchal upbringing rooted in the firm belief about the traditional role assigned to women as per his understanding of the ancient Indian scriptures. At another level Gandhi emerges as a social reformer concerned about the backwardness of women in India. In this *avatar* he champions the rights of women as equal partners of men. At still another level Gandhi sees women as a potential resource for the success of his movements, both political and social, and advocates their increased participation. Here too Gandhi's faith in women's power is born out of a deep spiritual understanding where he has the ideals of Sita or Savitri in mind. There are times when all the three levels merge; making his views on women an enigma.

The views of Gandhi on the women's question that irked the feminists especially are with regard to the duties he assigned to women in social life. Gandhi could not appreciate the fact of women working in factories to supplement the family income. He favoured their role as home-makers, taking care of family and children.[1] He wanted them to be educated but was against imparting English education to them. He believed that English education was of no use to them because it had no application in their day to day life.[2] In all fairness to Gandhi, it must be noted here that he considered English education as a wastage of time for the common people, the peasants and the artisans because it did not help them in their day to day life. He had no problems with regard to co-education but believed that once the gender relations are sorted out in the Indian family, co-education will follow as a natural consequence.[3] On purely spiritual and moral grounds he was against artificial means of birth control and especially against the use of contraceptives or abortions for the purpose. He preferred sexual continence to artificial methods of birth control. On being told that this was not possible in the situation in which women are placed in India he refused to believe that women are that powerless as not to have a say in the matter.[4] The same moral high ground was reflected in his advice to women who were molested during communal riots. He asked them to either kill the culprit or kill themselves.[5]

Psychologists have tried to unravel the source of Gandhi's seemingly patriarchal views. Erik Erikson has linked this to his marital experiences and the feelings of guilt about his natural sensual needs.[6] In the last phase of his life Gandhi conducted the highly controversial 'body experiments' in order to purify his mind of sensual desires. Though at personal level he was satisfied about his spiritual evolution such experiments were not appreciated by his colleagues and friends and at the insistence of Thakkar Bapa, a revered old friend, he dropped them. The deep influence of the Jain tradition which refers to the importance of the purity of the seeker of truth in order to attract similar vibrations around him motivated Gandhi to conduct such experiments. Gandhi had been deeply hurt by news of molestation of women during communal riots and had concluded that perhaps the impurity of his mind, the leader's mind, was responsible for such happenings.

As a social reformer, Gandhi included the work for uplift of women in his Constructive Programme. He repeatedly made it clear that women were in no way inferior to men and this canard has been spread through ancient writings whose authors were men.[7] In fact Gandhi went a step further and said that in terms of capacity to suffer and belief in nonviolence women were far superior to men.[8] He advocated education to empower them.[9] He asked them to be economically self-sufficient in order to maintain their dignity. He advised them to participate in social life and contribute to moral and spiritual growth of the community. He was against the *purdah* system that cut off women from social life.[10] He was also against dowry system and exhorted the youth not to ask for dowry in their marriages. Using very strong words he said, 'Any young man who makes dowry a condition of marriage discredits his education and his country and dishonours womanhood.'[11] He advocated remarriage for child widows but was not very forthcoming on the marriage of widows who had enjoyed a long married life.[12]

Gandhi believed in equal rights of both men and women. He also wanted women to be represented in proportion to their population in the legislatures and panchayats and had said that he would not like to be a member of a legislature where women were on represented.[13] It was no coincidence that Sarojini Naidu succeeded Gandhi as the President of the Congress Party and the Constituent Assembly that drafted the Constitution of India had sizeable number of woman who spoke on women issues.

As an astute strategist, Gandhi soon realized the potential of woman in contributing to the success of his movements. He tried this in South Africa where the government by a piece of legislation had declared all Indian marriages solemnized outside courts as illegal. Gandhi explained the implications of such a ruling to women and they spontaneously came out in large numbers protesting against the evil law. In India, initially Gandhi confined the role of women to picketing and similar non-aggressive activities during the Non-Cooperation Movement. Out of a sense of dignity, he believed that the English would not like to use force against women and he did not want to misuse this sensitivity for his personal gain. Later, however, during the Civil Disobedience Movement he encouraged women to take over leadership roles. The role of

Sarojini Naidu in the Dharasana Salt Depot raid during the Salt Satyagraha was reported the world over. Gandhi made it a point to report the non-violent exploits of the women leaders in the columns of his newspapers, eulogizing them in glowing terms. Women were at the forefront even in dousing communal fires. Amtulassalam accompanied Gandhi in the worst communal affected areas in Noakhali and went on fast for communal harmony.

To sum up one can say that Gandhi's views on women's question apparently appear very complex but if one goes deep into the origins of such beliefs one finds that they are born out of deep concern, respect and empathy for them. The most enlightened and forward looking women of the period, both Indian and foreign, were Gandhi's friends and confidantes. This would not have been possible had Gandhi been a close-minded man with patriarchal mind-set.

REFERENCES

1. MK Gandhi, *Hind Swaraj or Indian Home Rule*, p. 33.
2. *Harijan*, 27-2-37, in RK Prabu's compilation, *India of My Dreams*, p. 232.
3. *Harijan*, 9-11-47 in *Ibid.*, p. 233.
4. 'Interview of Margaret Sanger', *Harijan*, 21-1-36, *CWMG*, LXII, pp. 156-60.
5. 'Woman's Honour', *Harijan*, 14-1-40, in RK Prabu's compilation, *India of My Dreams*, p. 230.
6. Erikson Erik H.: *Gandhi's Truth: On the Origins of Militant Nonviolence*, Faber and Faber Limited, London, 1970, p. 97.
7. R.K. Prabhu, *op.cit.*, p. 227.
8. Talking to women workers late in April 1947, nine months before his assassination, Gandhi was confident that 'India can proclaim that she can defend herself and make progress not through the atom bomb but through non-violence alone' and that 'women alone can take the lead in this, for God had endowed them with great power. If women resolve to bring glory to the nation, within a few months they can totally change the face of the country because of the spiritual background of the Indian women.' *CWMG*, Vol. 87, pp. 250 & 294.
9. R.K. Prabhu *op. cit.*, 232-233.
10. *Ibid.*, p. 227.
11. *Ibid.*
12. *Ibid.* p. 226.
13. Statement made at Round Table Conference in 1931.

13
Relevance of Gandhi

Thirty-five years after the crucifixion of Jesus Christ there was no indication that Christianity would emerge as one of the great spiritual forces of history. Around 450 B.C., three decades after the death of Confucius, nobody could have predicted how influential his ideas eventually became. And around 1915, thirty years after Karl Marx, the Communist movement seemed doomed to be an inconsequential political aberration. Perhaps, then we are too near Gandhi to evaluate his impact on history.

— Ralph Buultjens in 1984 *(Buultjens is a professor at New York University, and the former Nehru Professor/Professorial Fellow at the University of Cambridge. He was awarded the Toynbee Prize for Social Sciences in 1984).*

The discussion on the relevance of Gandhi is not a matter of skepticism today; it is subject for recapitulation. Gandhi believed that moral values sustain human life and differentiate humans from animals. As Tushar Gandhi, one of the grandsons of Gandhi put it rhetorically, 'Is life relevant? Is truth relevant? Is morality relevant? It has become a fashion to question the relevance of Mahatma Gandhi today. I suspect the people who ask this question are the ones who are convinced that he is irrelevant and useless. I want to ask them if they feel life, truth and morality are also irrelevant? Because the cornerstones of the Gandhian philosophy are life, truth and morality.'[1]

Let us examine the relevance of some of the ideas of Gandhi in today's world.

Non-violence

Gandhi was one of the most ardent advocates of non-violence in the twentieth century. He had supreme faith in the power of non-violence to solve the most inscrutable problems of the day. He even advocated that the Jews should have offered nonviolent satyagraha before the Nazis.

Gandhi's insistence on non-violence is the most debatable issue today. It is said that in the present age of warfare and terrorism, nonviolent methods are ineffective. Tushar Gandhi, however, disagrees. According to him, in 'this age of nuclear weapons and the recently popularised term 'Weapons of Mass Destruction' the only philosophy or rather way of life that ensures our longevity on earth is nonviolence.' One may achieve temporary victories through violence but non-violent methods ensure lasting peace. To prove his point, Tushar Gandhi gives the examples from recent history such as the Irish settlement, the civil rights movement of the sixties in the US and the more recent Nelson Mandela's initiative through The Truth and Reconciliation Commission to bring the Blacks and the Whites together in the development of South Africa. On the other hand, a glaring failure of violent approach is America's war against terror. The Arab-Israeli confict all these years has only resulted in alienating both the parties. India and Pakistan also have started looking at alternatives other than war to resolve their mutual disputes. All these examples prove that dialogue, discussion and talks are better alternatives to war. In fact, they are the more effective and lasting alternatives.

A completely violence free world may not be possible but less and less use of violence would ensure better life for human beings. Even Gandhi permitted the use of violence in certain situations. He preferred violence to cowardice but he was against the use of violence to solve problems which could be solved through dialogues, appeal to conscience or other non-violent methods. Gandhi's statement: 'An eye for an eye only

'THE ODD THING ABOUT ASSASSINS, DR. KING, IS THAT THEY THEY THINK THEY'VE KILLED YOU."

ends up making the whole world blind', is s truism. If we believe that nonviolence is irrelevant we will leave behind a world on the verge of destruction caused by a mankind blinded by hatred and prejudice.

The issue that is raised in this context is whether it is possible to defend one's country against foreign attack in a non-violent manner? Gandhi had to face this dilemma in his lifetime. In 1947 the Pakistani troops attacked Jammu and Kashmir and the Indian army had to intervene on the request the of ruler of the state. Against this background the discussion between General Cariappa, the first Indian Chief of the Army Staff, and Gandhi is instructive. Cariappa had made a statement that 'Non-violence is of no use under the present circumstances in India and only a strong army can make India one of the greatest nations of the world.' When Gandhi read about this statement he wrote in his newspaper that the General should talk about military affairs alone and not dabble in matters over which he had no expertise. He who is an expert on non-violence, alone knew about its effectiveness.[1] The General took Gandhi's criticism in the right spirit and came to discuss the matter with him. The meeting was an amicable one in which Cariappa clarified that he, or soldiers for that matter, are the last ones to support war. They merely perform the duty of defending their country when they are asked to. Gandhi in response commended the army personnel for their sense of duty and discipline and asked Cariappa to come back to him after his visit to Jammu and Kashmir where he was proceeding for discussing ways and means of settling the issue. Gandhi also confessed to Cariappa that he was groping in the dark over the issue of war versus nonviolence. The promised meeting, however, did not materialize because by the time Cariappa returned from his talks on 30th January 1948, Gandhi had been shot dead.[2]

Around the same time there were reports in the newspapers, especially the foreign press that Gandhi advocated war against Pakistan. Clarifying his stand on the issue he said at a prayer meeting, 'What I said was that if Pakistan was committing mistakes or if India was committing mistakes, with both the countries having their own independent Governments, how was it possible for one Government to secure justice from another? It would be different if the two Governments worked in co-operation. Let them have an arbitrator if they cannot work together. If even that cannot be done, then we shall helplessly be dragged into war.'[3] This clearly was not an advocacy of the war but an effort to defuse the situation so that war did not take place.

India and Pakistan have gone to war four times till date and the problem of Jammu and Kashmir is nowhere near resolution. In fact, war has further embittered relations between the two neighbours. In the last ten years other means of resolving the dispute are being explored and with encouraging results.

A realization is dawning upon humanity that a war-less world is not impossible. Recently a retired American officer who had served in the American army during the Korean War and who is now a professor of Political Science has argued with the help of examples gleaned from all over the world that a non-killing society was indeed possible and that there are communities in the world today that have never indulged in killing each other or gone to war.[4]

The Gandhian way today

H.T 30.1.99

PODIUM

Gene Sharp

ON JANUARY 30, 1948, Mohandas K. Gandhi was assassinated. It is now fifty one years later. This is an appropriate time to reflect on what lessons his thought and actions have for us who face many acute conflicts throughout the world. These are often conflicts in which important issues related to freedom and justice are at stake.

What are Gandhi's lessons for us — we who suffer the combined pains of popular powerlessness and pervasive violence, and who will soon enter the twenty-first century? These appear to me as follows:

— Justice and freedom require empowering oppressed people and redistributing power in society.

— Peace is not achieved by stifling conflicts in which important issues are at stake but by using nonviolent struggle to fight out those conflicts to a resolution.

— Mass nonviolent struggle in politics is possible as a substitute both for passivity and for violence.

— Masses of people who will never accept nonviolence as a moral principle will at times practise pragmatic nonviolent struggle.

— The key to widespread adoption of nonviolent means lies in formulating and implementing strategies of nonviolent struggle to serve as substitutes for violence for specific purposes.

— Nonviolent struggles can be made significantly more effective if wise strategies with implementing tactics are developed and applied.

— Nonviolent struggle can be developed, refined, adapted, and adopted in a series of specific replacements to be a substitute for violence as the final means of applying pressure and power in society and politics.

Nonviolent struggle has existed for many centuries. Gandhi learned from some of those cases including those in Russia, China, England, South Africa, Bengal, Ireland and elsewhere.

We are now at a new stage in the development of nonviolent struggle. It is possible to refine this technique to make it more effective, to adapt it for use in several types of acute conflicts, and to increase the chances of success while reducing casualties.

A great deal of research, analysis, policy development, education, consulting and planning is required to explore and develop the potential of nonviolent action and to take action in the acute conflicts of our time. These include disintegrating dictatorships, blocking coups d'etat, resisting genocide, lifting oppression, and correcting economic injustices.

These efforts will require going beyond, and often against, important established trends of modern society and powerful national and international forces. The centralisation of power, the militarisation of inter-state politics, the hegemony of traditional methods of problem-solving — these and other factors work against reasoned consideration of the potential relevance of nonviolent struggle.

(Excerpted from a speech by Gene Sharp, senior scholar at the Albert Einstein Institution, USA, and author of Gandhi as a Political Strategist*)*

Satyagraha

Gandhi practised and advocated *satyagraha* as a means of fighting injustice of all kinds. Satyagraha was a duty as well as a right. It was every person's duty not to suffer injustice. It was every person's right to fight against every kind of injustice. The other party in the case could be a family member, one's community, one's government and so on. This fight was to be totally nonviolent and certain rules and regulations were strictly to be followed.[1] Scholars have recounted success stories of such *satyagraha* not only from India but from across the world.

Non-violent resistance was used by Norwegians during the Second World War; by the people of Czechosovakia in 1948; and the Poles under the leadership of Lech Walesa in the 1970s. Martin Luther King used the Gandhian method in his struggle for seeking equal status for Blacks in the USA in 1960s. In his book *Stride Towards Freedom* King has put down six principles of nonviolence which are the same as Gandhian principles of non-violence. King and his colleagues, showed their respect for Gandhi when they named the Education Fund which supported the Civil Rights Movement as the Gandhi Society for Human Rights. Inspired by King an institute is functioning in Atlanta (Georgia, USA) where non-violent method of policing is taught to police personnel.[5]

Gandhi had many adherents to his methods in the Continent of Africa as well. The African National Congress was unable to adhere to non-violence after the Sharpeville massacre of the sixties', but Nelson Mandela consciously adopted a policy of national conciliation in the spirit of Gandhi in the transition to multi-racial democratic system. Other African leaders, such as Kenneth Kaunda of Zambia and Nkrumah of Ghana, acknowledged their debt to Gandhi, while conducting their struggles against colonialism. The democratic movement in Philippines in 1996 was totally nonviolent where people organized a peace army after the fashion of Gandhi's Shanti Sena. In the concept of Shanti Sena the West has found an inspiration for a Global International Peace Force which came into existence after the Hague Appeal for Peace in 1999.The Tian-An Men Square movement in China (1989) was also nonviolent though the Chinese have no great tradition of non-violence. In Myannmar Aung San Su Ki's movement against repressive regime is totally nonviolent and so was the 'peace walk' in Cambodia protesting against the authoritarian regime in 1990. Michael True, an American scholar, has listed at least 23 books and articles on nonviolent methods as alternative to violence apart from eight journals devoted exclusively to the propagation of nonviolence in the world today.[6] The *Times* named Gandhi the Man of the Year in 1930, the runner-up to Albert Einstein; as 'Person of the Century' at the end of 1999; and named the Dalai Lama, Lech Walêsa, Dr. Martin Luther King, Jr., Cesar Chavez, Aung San Suu Kyi, Benigno Aquino, Jr., Desmond Tutu, and Nelson Mandela as *Children of Gandhi* and his spiritual heirs to non-violence.

The human rights activists have found a wealth of methods in which to carry on their struggles nonviolently. Gene Sharp, an American professor specializing in Gandhian methods, has recounted how in different parts of the world nonviolent struggles have been used to undermine dictatorships and prevent new ones; to defeat coup-de -etat ; deter and resist foreign aggression ; to aid struggles of indigenous peoples; to advance social justice; to preserve and extend democratic processes and human rights throughout the world.[7] Gene Sharp has also written at great length on Gandhi as an astute strategist. According to him, *satyagraha,* even without its strict moral code, could be adopted as a useful strategy and prove as effective.[8] Aldous Huxley was not wrong when he predicted way back in 1946 that 'in the year ahead it seems possible that satyagraha may take root in the West, not primarily as the result of any "change of heart", but simply because it provides the masses, especially in the conquered countries, with their only practical form of political action.'[9] His famous essay published in 1946 entitled *Science, Liberty and Peace,* is filled with insights about the connections between science, violence and nonviolence. Huxley believed that nonviolence was the only way forward. He saw hope in Gandhi's methods. K.Natwar Singh, the former Foreign Secretary of India, is not off the mark when he commented that 'Gandhi's concept of creative nonviolent, non-co-operation—Satyagraha—is the only political idea to come out from Asia, Africa and Latin America in the past 300 years.'[10]

Swaraj[11]

Swaraj is a multilayered concept used by Gandhi. It stands for independence from foreign rule (national independence);

political liberties and democratic governance; economic equality; and, last but not least, self control. This is a unique concept in so far as there is no equivalent to this concept in western thought. Gandhi's concept of rights or freedoms was different from the western concept in the sense that he laid great emphasis on duties. Without corresponding duties, Gandhi believed that rights might degenerate into license. The absence of violence in gaining these rights was also an important feature of the Gandhian concept of political freedom. If another person or state snatches away one's rights Gandhi insisted on nonviolent satyagraha through self-suffering rather than taking to violence. The first part of his formulation in emphasizing performance of duties is significant today as rights have indeed been used as license, especially in the matter of freedom of expression thereby taking away similar right of the other. In the other sphere – of launching *satyagraha* – it is even today resorted to in cases where citizens feel that their rights are not protected by the state. The movements for right to information, protection of environment fall under this category.

Swaraj as *freedom from economic deprivation* underlines the farsightedness of Gandhi who very rightly saw that without economic equality, other rights would be more or less ineffective. The poorest must receive the necessities of life before the rich get excess wealth. He believed that economic *swaraj* could be ensured through the use of indigenously produced goods which are used and consumed at local level. Economic *swaraj* was also ensured by sustainable development and appropriate technology which was environment-friendly as well as capable of giving employment to people. These insights are very relevant in India today which is facing both environmental degradation as well as poverty due to wrong economic policies and planning.

Gandhi's idea of *swaraj,* unlike the communists' ideal of liberation, *did not see the rich and poor classes as antagonistic to each other.* Though he wanted the eradication of poverty and restoration of the dignity of labour, he considered revolution undesirable for gaining these ends. In India today we still battle with the problem of Naxalites and see them as enemies of establishment without addressing the root cause of the problem.

Gandhi's doctrine of *Trusteeship* was a novel idea to resolve the rich-poor divide. According to him the rich are merely trustees of the wealth they hold because in the creation of this wealth the workers have also participated. It is, therefore, the duty of the rich to set aside a part of their wealth for philanthropic purposes. In one of his addresses at Gandhi Smriti in 2005, BG Verghese, the well known journalist, stated that the idea of Trusteeship was akin to the present idea of *Corporate Social Responsibility,* where the corporate sector is asked to take up socially useful programmes for the community outside their industry.

While Gandhi asked the rural rich to share their lands with the landless, later taken up by Gandhi's disciple, Vinoba Bhave as the *Bhoodan Movement,* he suggested to the industrialists to allow *workers participation in management.* This is how he resolved the famous Ahmedabad Mill workers strike in 1918. He also *supported the right of the workers to strike for just cause and in a nonviolent manner.* His conduct of the Ahmedabad Mill Workers strike of 1918 is a case study in the resolution of industrial disputes in the most amicable manner, while defending the rights of the workers. The present day strikers could learn a lesson or two from this epic strike.

Swaraj also means *self-control.* Only a country that is peopled by men and women of character can take it forward. This self rule is not selfish but expressed through the service of the community. It is the self rule/control of a *karmayogi.* Character is ensured through *value based education* where students are also taught community service and importance of bread labour. The schools are institutions that teach pupils and prepare them to be self-sufficient, capable of earning their livelihood. The need for value based education cannot be denied in today's world. Similarly linking education of with livelihood is recognized by even the Supreme Court of India today in its interpretation of the Right to Life and Personal Liberty.(Article 21 of the Constitution)

Abolition of Untouchability

Gandhi made the issue of the eradication of untouchability the central point of his movement for *swaraj*. As long as a section of people were treated as untouchables, real *swaraj* was a distant dream. It was a bold move for he was going against the entrenched beliefs of the powerful section of traditional co-religionists. He asked Sanskrit scholars to come up with a strong condemnation of untouchability. Even if it were mentioned in some religious books, he exhorted Hindus to condemn it as an inhuman practice. Any person who believed in untouchability could not become a member of the Congress Party, or participate in any movement launched by Gandhi.

Gandhi supported and encouraged laws to abolish untouchability. He strongly recommended Dr. Ambedkar's name for the chairmanship of the Constituent Assembly so that the Dalit sensibilities could be reflected in our Constitution. He advocated change of mindset instead of reservation for the resolution of the problem. It is clear after 60 years of independence that this was the real cure for the malaise. Satish Deshpande, the well-known sociologist, has remarked how for the enlightened Indians caste is invisible whereas for others it is the only reality[12] because they are the perpetrators and the victims of this mindset.

Sarvodaya and Swadeshi

The greatest happiness of the greatest number was not the goal of Gandhi. He wanted the greatest happiness of/for *all*. As referred to earlier, he wanted the basic needs of all to be satisfied before the extra needs of some was fulfilled. The Gandhian *talisman* with which every school-going child is familiar in India, is a constant reminder of what Gandhi wanted Indians to keep in mind.

Gandhi is generally accused of glorifying poverty; this has no merit. If Gandhi maintained a life similar to that of the poor in India, it was a penance on his part for not being able to ensure the comforts of the rich to the poor. Gandhi had some practical suggestions in the matter. Propagation of handicrafts and spinning was one way of providing employment to all. The idea was symbolic. Gandhi was *dead against the use of machinery that would replace human labour*. He wanted the introduction of *suitable technology of development* in India that could provide jobs to the people and not take away their jobs. He wanted some structural reforms in the economic system whereby every village became self-sufficient and after its needs were met, to be able to give away its spare products to cities or other villages. To this date this simple formula of Gandhi has not been employed and the amount of grain that is wasted in pooling it in the central pool and then redistributing it to the villages is enough to feed whole of the population living below the poverty line.[13]

Human Rights

Gandhi's contribution to Human Rights is recognized the world over. Atrocities committed during the Second World War drew the attention of the right thinking people in the direction of having a bill of rights applicable to all countries of the world. Mrs Eleanor Roosevelt, the widow of US President FD Roosevelt, took initiative in this direction. She sent elaborate questionnaires to the heads of states in Europe seeking their opinion in the matter. She also sought opinion from Chinese, Islamic and Hindu leaders to get their perspective. Mahatma Gandhi was also consulted because his activities in South Africa were acknowledged as fit examples of human rights initiatives and were an inspiration for the human rights activists in the world. Even today, Gandhi is considered to be the 'originator and the most influential exponent of human rights of the 20th century.'[14]

The Universal Declaration of Human Rights (December 10, 1948) contains rights to life, liberty and security of person; prohibits slavery, cruel or degrading treatment; entitles everyone the right to recognition everywhere as person before law with right to equality before law and equal protection against any discrimination; freedom from arbitrary arrest; right to family and privacy; right to nationality; right to various freedoms like freedom of expression, assembly, participation in government and public service; right to work, health, education and participation in cultural life and so on.

Gandhi's public life was a shining example of his commitment to these rights before they were even articulated. Gandhi had raised his voice against racialism in South Africa. He sought equality for the so-called 'untouchables' in India. He had argued for the rights of indigo farmers in Bihar. He had gone on fast when a wage claim for textile workers in Ahmedabad was unjustly rejected. He had dared the British to confer self-rule to Indians and leave the country. He had protested nonviolently against the massacre in Jallianwallah. He had condemned oppression of women and the poor. He had worked tirelessly for respect of religious freedom. He was instrumental in drafting a bill of rights as early as 1931 in the Congress Session at Karachi which was a model for the Fundamental Rights later incorporated in the Constitution of independent India.

Gandhi was not an armchair theorist on human rights but was a full time activist working in the field. As a observer has commented 'Gandhi practised human rights as no man or woman has before or since.' Today when the record of human rights is very dismal throughout the world Gandhi has become all the more relevant. His methods and strategies need to be studied and practised.

Gandhi's attitude towards or views on Human Rights were however very different from the Western thinking on Human Rights. In her essay 'Gandhi and Human Rights: In Search of True Humanity' Judith Brown cautions those who try to appropriate Gandhi as a defender of Human Rights. Brown focuses on some of Gandhi's key thoughts revolving around *dharma* (duty). Though Gandhi received a western legal education and had great admiration for such western thinkers as Tolstoy, Ruskin, and Thoreau, his thinking was not founded upon western liberal human rights discourses centralized on the freedoms of individuals but, upon Indian philosophical traditions conceptually grounded to protect the community as a whole. Gandhi's worldview emphasized dharma—as performance of our duties to the people around us—as a path to achieve true *swaraj*. According to Gandhi, people have no natural individual rights, only those rights that were earned through their performance of duty.

The appropriation of Gandhi for human rights causes, according to Brown, is based on a simplified picture of Gandhi's thought (and his life) which, if more closely studied, shows us that Gandhi's had different goals for humanity than human rights proponents. 'For them rights are the device for protecting core values and attributes of individual and group life, vis-à-vis the forces of the state and society. For him recognition of individual duty and social and moral interdependence were the foundation of an authentic human existence', writes Brown.[15] Gandhi clearly thought that for the majority of the world's peoples 'Human Rights' in the western sense were unattainable until the method in which the wealthy minority lived changed. Thus a clearer assessment of the relationship between western thought and Gandhi can begin when Gandhi's ideas are understood in their own context and not just as an extension of the western intellectual tradition.

Gandhi's Religion

Gandhi's concept of religion was very practical and more suited to the present times. Though himself a devout Hindu, he was open to the teachings of other faiths. Religion for him was a personal matter, something as he put it 'between me and my maker'. In the public sphere he followed the religion of humanity, a 'religion which was above all religions'. At his prayer meetings recitations from religious books of different faiths were made. Even at the height of communal tension he did not give up this practice.

Gandhi's religion demanded strict standards of morality in personal life. His religion did not advocate running away from the world. It enjoined him to stay in the midst of the world with a detached mind and serve the poor and the downtrodden in society. It was a religion of service and compassion. He was a *karmayogi* who worked relentlessly for the sick, the poor and the deprived. For Gandhi 'God was Truth'. He later went on to describe 'Truth' as 'God' which made some wonder whether he had turned an atheist.

Gandhi seldom visited temples. He was put off by the unhygienic conditions in some of these. Another reason was that since most of these temples did not allow the so called untouchables' entry he did not visit them.

In the present context when religion is the dividing force in the world and in India, Gandhi's views acquire significance. He was bold enough to point out the illogical and inhuman aspects of religions and ask people to judge them on the touchstone of compassion and humanity and not blindly follow them. By his own admission in this respect he was an 'iconoclast'.

Journalistic Ethics

Media and press are important opinion makers and influencer of public opinion in the present times. In this context Gandhi's views on the role and responsibility of the media need to be studied.

Gandhi was a journalist of first order. His impact on journalism was so far-reaching that his advent in journalism was hailed as 'not mere an event but a phenomenon.'[16] Gandhi's journalistic career spanned nearly half a century. Beginning with his unpublished *London Diary (*written in 1889) his first publications were a series of articles published in *The Vegetarian,* the journal of the Vegetarian Society of England (between 1891-95). These attempts have been noticed only in retrospect. What established Gandhi as a journalist, however, was his editorship of the weekly *Indian Opinion* (since 1904) published from South Africa. On his return to India in 1915 Gandhi was already a known figure because of his fame as an activist journalist through the columns of *Indian Opinion* and his well-known *Green Pamphlet* on the condition of Indians in

South Africa. The infamous Rowlatt Act curbing the freedom of Indians gave birth to a new 'avatar' of journalist Gandhi. As an act of defiance to the provisions of the Act Gandhi started an unregistered weekly named *Satyagraha*. This was followed by *Young India* in English and *Navajivan* in Gujarati which were considered as his 'viewspapers' rather than newspapers.

In the thirties Gandhi started what is now known as his career in social journalism which the publication of *Harijan, Harijan Sewak* and *Harijanbandhu* in English, Hindi and Gujarati respectively. Through these newspapers Gandhi conducted his movements, informed public about their rights and duties, and gave suggestions on personal and public matters.

What is more important is the type of journalism Gandhi pursued. He used simple language to communicate his thoughts, did not resort to sensationalism, verified facts before publishing a report and did not accept advertisements for the fear that these could affect the impartiality of his newspapers. Gandhi was very particular about the duties of a journalist which are quoted as the model code even by journalists today. According to him 'one of the objects of a newspaper is to understand the popular feeling and give expression to it; another is to arouse in the people certain desirable sentiments, and the third is fearlessly to expose popular defects.' Referring to this statement in his Durga Das Memorial lecture the former President of India, Dr KR Narayanan had said, 'There are more modern statements of Western journalists that I could quote, but I know of no statement that has spelt out so clearly and succinctly the role and duties of a journalist as this one.'[17]

Gandhi's impact on journalism and literature has been immense. His writings in Gujarati freed Gujarati of its old stylized form. Gandhi made it more of a common man's language.[18] Similarly other regional languages also saw the merit of using unembellished and less pompous style. Munshi Prem Chand, one of the most popular of Hindi writers, chose to write in simple Hindustani, and not Sanskritised Hindi as some of his contemporaries did. His stories and writings show a distinct stamp of Gandhian ideas of truth, honesty and concern for the problems of the poor. Poets and writers took up issues of poor. Even Rabindra Nath Tagore whose writings were mainly spiritually oriented or related to nature wrote a poem on the 'Scavenger'. Social concerns became the theme of many of the writings that followed the Gandhian era.

Morality in Politics

For Gandhi politics was not for gaining power but for serving the people. On the eve of independence he advised the Congress party to disband and convert itself into Lok Seva Dal. These extreme views were influenced by Gandhi's experience of rule by Indians in British states after 1937. He found some of these governments suffering from the same malaise that afflicted their British predecessors and therefore was wary of power. Gandhi laid emphasis on high degree of probity in public life. Gandhi's influence was evident in our leaders who led the country after independence. Gradually the canker of corruption set in. Now India has the dubious distinction of being the fifth most corrupt country in the world, and the general perception of the rulers being a corrupt lot, *yatha raja, thatha praja* ('as is the ruler so are the subject') appears to be a truism for India. With development held hostage to corruption, the public is getting aware of its rights and the deep connection between morality and politics is being recognized. A respected politician and former Governor of Jammu and Kashmir, Sh Jagmohan reiterated the stand of Gandhi when he wrote: 'By not following Gandhi's interpretation of religion and by despiritualising politics, the present day world is merely adding to its sickness and reinforcing its hidden inhumanities Unfortunately, it is ignoring Gandhi's warning that "politics bereft of principles are death-traps; they kill the soul of a nation.'[19]

On the Role and Responsibility of Civil Society

Early in his life Gandhi was distrustful of the State as the state he encountered was the oppressive British State. Gandhi wrote, 'The individual has a soul but the State is a soulless machine, it can never be weaned from violence to which it owes its very existence.' In his conception of a nonviolent society, the state did not exist. A nonviolent state was a contradiction in terms. If nonviolence was to be the governing principle of society, one could not call it a state—it could be only called a nonviolent stateless society. Such a society was the Gandhian concept of an ideal state. In such a society people would grow accustomed spontaneously to observe their social obligations without the operation of the state.

While in the ideal society of Gandhi there is no room for the military and the police, yet in the actual state there is a provision for it according to the moral level of its citizens. That is to say, a predominantly non-violent state is a practical possibility and is the second best ideal of Gandhi. Gandhi's actual state does concede the desirability of using the military and police to deal with anti-social elements and defend the country. This concession, however, does not mean that he admitted to the weakness of the doctrine of nonviolence or *satyagraha*. He firmly believed that the fault or weakness lies in the people who practise it. As the people evolve morally so will the institutions evolve, or be replaced by better institutions. As distinct from the Marxian concept the Gandhian State does not 'wither away' but evolves into a moral state and its institutions evolve accordingly. Unlike the anarchists the state does not move towards statelessness but towards an ethical and moral order. Unlike the liberals the state does not take up the responsibility of its citizens but helps them to be self-reliant. Only in such a state can people be truly free.

Gandhi did not live to realize his dream of an ideal or predominantly nonviolent state but he managed to concretize a Gandhian vision of State in which human beings and not institutions are the ultimate consideration. The following are some of its features;—

1. Political decentralization in the form of direct participatory democracy operating in a tier structure from base village level tier upward through the district

and state and then the national, and ultimately, international level.

2. Economic decentralization with distribution of wealth, and with villages as basic economic units
3. Minimization of competition and exploitation in the economic sphere. This is reflected in the idea of Trusteeship whereby the rich would act as trustees of their properties rather than their owners (partially recognized today as Corporate Social Responsibility)
4. Production and consumption on the basis of need rather than greed. All must have the basic necessities of life before some have more than what is required.
5. Recognition of dignity of labour and greater purity of village life, that is, living a life close to and in harmony with nature.
6. Emphasis on individual, village and national self reliance (Swadeshi).
7. Absence of oppression on the basis of race, caste, class, language, gender or religion.
8. A deep respect for nature, necessitating an economic system based on preservation rather than destruction of the natural environment (sustainable development).

Gandhi seldom used the word 'state' for India. Neither did he use the word 'nation'. He used the terms 'swaraj', 'swadeshi', 'Indian civilization' or 'sarvodaya' singularly or collectively to describe what we now know as his concept of state.

It is clear from Gandhi's description of state that he sought to widen the jurisdiction of civil society and proportionately limit the jurisdiction of the state. He had serious misgivings about the symbols of state power—the police, the army and the bureaucracy. His emphasis on self-control was motivated by the idea of lessening the need of police in the civil sphere. In his life time Gandhi was successful to a great extent in developing a civil society in India which would help realize his ideal state or 'Ram Rajya'. Even today this civil society is active in protesting and organizing movements against the highhandedness of the state. In the field of environment, protection of civil liberties, personal freedoms, rights of women, children, dalits, the handicapped, the elderly, inhuman treatment of animals—it is the civil society that has taken up cudgels against the symbols of state power. The noted human rights activist of Pakistan, Asma Jehangir has praised the Indian civil society for its role in limiting state power.

In the light of the above discussion it becomes clear that Gandhi's views, far from being irrelevant, have become in some cases, the only alternative to the crisis the world is facing today. The whole confusion about the relevance of Gandhi stems from the fact that people fail to distinguish between Gandhi the man, Gandhism as a set of doctrines; and the activities of Gandhians since Gandhi's death. Gandhi had very clearly stated: 'There is no such thing as "Gandhism," and I do not want to leave any sect after me. I do not claim to have originated any new principle of doctrine. I have simply tried in my own way to apply the eternal truths to our daily life and problems. Truth and non-violence are as old as the hills. All I have done is to try experiments in both on as vast a scale as I could do. In doing so I have sometimes erred and learnt by my errors. Life and its problems have thus become to me so many experiments in the practice of truth and non-violence.'[20]

Gandhi as a man never claimed infallibility. He was ever ready to accept criticisms to his views and change accordingly if convinced that he was in the wrong. He was also aware and wary of the 'ism' that was coming up in his name and candidly confessed that he did not subscribe to 'Gandhism', which was promoted as an answer to all the ills prevailing in the society. The followers of Gandhi also contributed to the confusion by the variety of interpretations they gave to Gandhi's thought. Some followed Gandhi in spirit while others paid only lip service to his philosophy of life. Gandhi can therefore be best understood and his relevance best assessed if and when he is read in original and in the context in which he was writing.

SUNDAY HINDUSTAN TIMES
OCTOBER 2, 2005

Gandhiji on Kashmir

He would have played the part of an advisor and ensured the discontent in J&K didn't brew for 5 decades

A CORRESPONDENT from Delhi has asked whether I welcome these talks. Believe me, I am as impatient as you are that these talks go forward. But the talks will achieve little as long as they concentrate on grievances and their redressal. To talk only of justice is a thoughtless and angry outburst whether it comes from Indians, Pakistanis or Kashmiris. 'Might is right' is the last word of justice and nothing but justice. When we come to a settlement, as we shall some day, we will not weigh it on the so-called scales of justice. But we shall have introduced in the calculation the disturbing factor of surrender, otherwise called love or affection or fellow feeling. And so will it be with us in India and Pakistan when we have killed each other in sufficient numbers and realised our foolishness. The scales will then fall from our eyes and we shall recognise that not justice but surrender and nothing but surrender was the law of friendship. When that happy day arrives, we shall know each other's virtues. Our vices will not obtrude themselves upon our gaze. I hope that day will come soon.

— *As imagined by Sudhir Kakar*

GANDHIJI WAS never in the Government. He had no magic wand. The weapon he had was advice — whether spoken or written. He would have used persuasion to try and solve the J&K dispute. If he had been there, such discontent wouldn't have been there and the dispute wouldn't have dragged on for 40-50 years. He wasn't weak — when he proposed a course of action, he stuck to it.

— *B R Nanda*

THE INVASION of Kashmir happened in Gandhiji's lifetime and he supported India sending its armed forces to defend Kashmir against raiders. Gandhiji's approach to what is now referred to as the 'Indo-Pak problem' would have been to try to solve the problems between the two nations on the basis of respect and regard for each other and each other's interests, trying to understand what the other party is saying.

He would have given this advice to both sides and would have tried and help develop trust and regard for each other.

— *Bipin Chandra*

Gandhiji and the iPod

Deliberate and voluntary reduction of wants alone promotes happiness

AN OLD friend asks whether I am not appalled by the consumption frenzy of our middle class countrymen who have shed all inhibitions in the pursuit of possessions.

Now, I am an admirer of the Indian middle class, of its energy and its drive. I only wish the energy were better directed. To me, anything we possess without needing it is stolen property. In India, we have millions of people who have to be satisfied with one meal a day, which consists of a *chappati* with no fat and a pinch of salt. You and I have no right to anything we have unless these millions are clothed and fed better. If each retained possession only of what he needed, no one would be in want. As matters stand, the rich, who want to be richer, are as discontented as the poor who want to be rich. Civilisation consists not in multiplication but in the deliberate and voluntary reduction of wants. This alone promotes happiness. I wish our middle class would direct its considerable energy in examining the nature of its desires than in the acquisition of desire's objects.

— *As imagined by Sudhir Kakar*

Gandhiji and a nuclear India

Indians need spiritual training that leads to fearlessness so that they have no reason to fear foreign bullies

MY ONLY criterion here is whether the acquisition of nuclear weapons will make Indians fearless. Whether it will make them stand up, not to other countries, but to the injustice and oppressors within their own land. If the answer is yes, then I welcome nuclear or any other weapons. But I suspect the answer is "No".

We know that the vast majority of Indians, the Hindus, are a gentle people who over the centuries, have become docile to the point of timidity. Cowardice is a natural excrescence of gentleness. Donning armor does not make a child a man. It may even harm him by giving him the illusion of power he does not have. For imbuing fearlessness, I would restore the spiritual culture we once had but have lost. The best and most lasting self-defense is self-purification and not nuclear weapons. I refuse to be lifted off my feet by the scares that haunt us today. If Indians would but believe in themselves, go through the spiritual training that leads to fearlessness, they will have no reason to fear bullying by any other country.

— *As imagined by Sudhir Kakar*

Gandhiji and Usama

Nothing is achieved through violence. Explain to the terrorists that their methods mar their cause

THE WAR is over in Afghanistan and Iraq but nothing has been solved. People say non-violence takes a long time, but can't solve anything through violence. The Gandhi way would be to see the enemy as a potential friend and non-violence as a means to conflict resolution. For that, everybody has to be willing to place their cards on the table and see how far they can go together. But there is anger and burden of the past.

— *BR Nanda, India's foremost Gandhi scholar*

GANDHIJI WOULD not only oppose the use of terror to achieve any objective but would also say that terror is resorted to when one is not able to build a majority or a large-scale public opinion. This is why he criticised revolutionaries like Bhagat Singh. Though he agreed with their objectives and also admired them, he insisted on the building of mass public opinion and support. He was not in favour of the basic tenets of terrorism — that a small minority tries to achieve an objective by terrorising others, be they outsiders or insiders. Terror should be dealt with by explaining to the terrorists that your cause is harmed by what you do. But in the event that this were not a possible or plausible route, he would warrant the use of the might of the State.

— *Bipin Chandra, eminent historian*

REFERENCES

1. Tushar Gandhi 'Is Mahatma Gandhi relevant today?', htpp://sify.com/news/ fullstory.
2. 'Outside his Field', *CWMG*, Vol.LXXXIX, p. 492.
3. For details of this meeting read Lalit Mohan, 'The Sage and the Soldier', *The Tribune*, 2 October, 2005.
4. *Ibid.*, 'Speech at a Prayer Meeting' , p. 252.
5. Glenn D.Paige, *Nonkilling Global Political Science*, Gandhi Media Centre, New Delhi,2002.
6. As already discussed in the chapter on satyagraha.
7. Confirmed by Charles I Alphin, in his paper 'Kingian Non-violence: Apractical Application in Policing', presented at the Seminar on Gandhi and Martin Luther King at Interenation Centre of Gandhian Studies and Research, Gandhi Smriti and Darshan Samiti, New Delhi, Decembet 1-2, 1997.
8. Michael True, 'The Story of Global Nonviolence Since 1989', International Peace Research Association, USA, 1995.
9. Gene Sharp, 'The Political Development of Non-violent Struggle: Past and Future', paper presented at workshop at Gandhi Smriti and Darshan Samiti, New Delhi, September 18-19, 1998.
10. For details read Gene Sharp, *Gandhi as a Political Strategist* Porter Sargent Publsihers, Boston, USA, 1979.
11. Aldous Huxley, *Science, Liberty and Peace,*New York: Harper & Row, 1946; London: Chatto & Windus, 1947. It has been reprinted by the A. J. Muste Memorial Institute, 339 Lafayette Street, New York NY 10012, USA.
12. K. Natwar Singh, 'The Eternal Pilgrim', *The Hindustan Times*, 30.1.98, p. 13.
13. For a useful discussion on the meaning of swaraj read AJ Parel, 'Gandhian Freedoms and Self-Rule' , in AJ Parel (edited), *Gandhi, Freedom, and Self-Rule*, vistaar Publications, New Delhi, 2002, pp. 1-23.
14. Satish Deshpande, 'Learning to Speak Caste', *The Times of India*,3 May, 2007.
15. Report in the *Hindustan Times*, 12.5.07.
16 Peter Townsend in his essay contributed to the Human Rights Balloon Debate :who is the greatest of the twentieth century?, Old Theatre, LSE, December 8, 2005.
17. Judith M Brown, 'Gandhi and Human Rights: In Search of True Humanity', in Anthony J Parel, *Gandhi, Freedom, and Self-Rule*, Vistaar Publications, New Delhi,2002, p.100.
18. R.C.S Sarkar, *The Press in India*, 1984, p. 28.
19. K.R. Narayanan, 'A Distorting Magnifying Mirror', *The Hindustan Times*, April 28, 1997.
20. K.M. Munshi, *Gujarati and its Literature*, (With Foreword by Gandhi)

Longmans, Green and Co. Ltd, Calcutta, 1935.

21. Jagmohan, 'Gandhi and the Removal of Spiritual Illiteracy', *The Hindustan Times*, 3.10.97.
22. *Harijan*, 28-3.'36.

The Epilogue

Looking back at the whole exercise Gandhi emerges as a political thinker whose ideas were not only responses to the conditions in which he lived but also the result of a deep analysis and a study of the perennial questions of philosophy. The conventional view treated Gandhi as a political activist with moral leanings. Even today scholars treat him at best as a political thinker rather than a contributor to political philosophy. AJ Parel's study of the historical and more importantly, the intellectual roots of Gandhi's writings present a yet unexplored area of Gandhi's thought process. Gandhi's engagement with the philosophical traditions of his times, his ingenuity in adapting those to his philosophy and the result that emerges in the shape of new innovations by Gandhi such as his doctrine of satyagraha, trusteeship and also his foresight in assessing the damaging effects of science and technology, erosion of moral values are not matters that could have emerged from an ordinary mind responding only to the circumstances of his times.

Those familiar with Gandhi's writings know that Gandhi was very particular with his choice of words and his writings are almost un-paraphrasable. Yet in the course of the previous discussion we find how different meanings are given to his writings and how they are used by people belonging to a range of ideologies in support of their views. Gandhi makes the work all the more difficult by changing his statements as he advances in age and maturity. Hence, those who look for consistency in his writings and statements are flabbergasted. His rejection as a political philosopher owes largely to this tendency. Gandhi, therefore, proves Quentin Skinner right about the fallacy of looking for consistency in a thinker and then dumping him just because he does not fit into the scheme of ideas supposedly attributed to him. Gandhi's Hind Swaraj *also shows how important is author's intention in judging his work, as emphasized by Skinner. The 'text in context' study of* Hind Swaraj *has helped clear many misunderstandings about it. But the same book also shows the inadequacy of Skinner's approach. The abiding interest in Hind Swaraj is not because of the 'intention' of the author but because of the perennial questions it seeks to answer. The renewed interest in the booklet in the Interwar years and in the present age of war, strife and introspection, points to the "problem driven" approach to the text, as stated by Terence Ball.*

At first sight, to subject Gandhi's writings to a scrutiny of difficult approaches seems to be an exercise in intellectual conceit. The simple man and his simple words, it is feared, should not have been subjected to such 'tortures'. Yet it should be borne in mind that Gandhi is now a world figure. He cannot escape being interpreted and re-interpreted, adopted and denounced, revered and mocked at. The best one can do in such a situation is to be as objective as possible in one's assessment while not maintaining a closed mind to the plethora of assessments.

While Anthony Parel's account gives a thorough background of the writing of Hind Swaraj *and some of the other significant works of Gandhi, Bhikhu Parekh gives a somewhat critical assessment of Gandhi. Interestingly, Parekh not only happens to be an Indian but one who belongs to Gandhi's home-state, Gujarat. Parekh also provides the readers with a new perspective on Gandhi pointing out the deep philosophical roots of his writings. David Hardiman, who is a serious researcher of the grass-root movements in Gujarat gives credit to Gandhi for some of his innovations at the lowest level and for alleviating the miseries of the poorest of the poor. He also appreciates the 'dialogic' process adopted by Gandhi and goes on to show the application of this approach in various ideas and movements of Gandhi. His assessment of Gandhi's 'inclusive nationalism' is also novel. In a way, Hardiman's characterization of Gandhi's critique of modernity as 'alternative modernity' is just one step behind Rudolphs' description of Gandhi as a 'postmodernist.'*

The discussion on Gandhi's critique of modernity, satyagraha and its relevance for modern times, his idea of nationalism, views on untouchability, status of women and his ingenious idea of religion – all have relevance for the present generation who has unfortunately seen only the caricature of Gandhi in most of their leaders. Gandhi's critique of modernity provides a thinking point for those who want to know where we are heading, and, whether the near perfect arrangement for bodily comforts has given us that elusive joy and contentment or not. Satyagraha has become a curiously popular theme in the present world and Gandhi is treated as 'cool' by the youth on this account.

As against the world-wide re-visitation of ethnic and nationalistic sentiments for a lost generation looking for its roots and sense of belonging, Gandhi's idea of nation appears very apt; it neither stifles nor uproots. The same can be said about the Gandhian idea of religion based on human values and compassion and yet strongly iconoclastic when placed against unreasonable doctrines. Gandhi's emphasis on the change of mindset and not cosmetic change alone has relevance for the themes of communal unity and abolition of untouchability. His emphasis on "heart unity" as the only way to unite people has been a model, the world over. The only area where Gandhi remains an enigma even today is with regard to his views on women. Gandhi on the one hand, supported the equal status of women, yet with regard to employment, he was not very confident that women could handle the conventional jobs of men. Similarly his views on marriage and sex may not find favour with the youth of today and may appear very outdated and ludicrous in the present age. Gandhi's deep respect for women led him at times to be overprotective about them. Similarly his interpretation of the Indian spiritual tradition as stating that bodily lust was a hindrance in the way of spiritual evolution led to the curious views about women. On these points, the debate on Gandhi is bound to continue.

J M Doke, the first biographer of Gandhi,[1] *had said that conversation with Gandhi was a lesson in liberal education. His life inspires many even today. Gandhi is not, to borrow Rudolphs' phrase, a 'backnumber'. His simple, practical solutions to everyday problems are worth emulating. A sample of this was shown in the vastly popular Bollywood film Munnabhai Lage Raho. The film highlighted how*

Gandhi interacted with people and helped them solve their everyday problems while not compromising on their values. In his lifetime Gandhi did this through the columns of his newspapers whereas in the film FM radio programme was used for the purpose. The interrelatedness of the individual spiritual quest and its impact on society was amply demonstrated by Gandhi through his life and activities. Gandhi emphatically brought home the fact that morals are not impractical ideals but something that can be practised in everyday life by anyone determined to do so.

REFERENCES

1. The material contained in the book by J. M. Doke, *M.K.Gandhi: A Patriot in South Africa* , Publications Division, Government of India, New Delhi, 2000.,was first published in *The London Chronicle* in 1909. The first Indian edition was brought out in 1919. Doke wrote, 'He is one of those outstanding characters with whom to talk was liberal education , whom to know is love'. p. 13.

Appendix–I

Gandhi's 11 Vows

- Ahimsa – Non-violence
- Satya – Truth
- Asteya – Non-stealing
- Brahmacharya – Self-discipline
- Aparigraha – Non-possession
- Sharirashrama – Bread labour
- Aswada – Control of the Palate
- Sarvatrabhayavarjana – Fearlessness
- Sarva Dharma Samatva – Equality of all religions
- Swadeshi – use locally made goods
- Sparshbhavana – Remove Untouchability

Appendix–II

CONSTRUCTIVE PROGRAMME
It's Meaning and Place

By M K Gandhi

INTRODUCTION

The constructive programme may otherwise and more fittingly be called construction of *Poorna Swaraj* or complete Independence by truthful and non-violent means.

Effort for construction of, Independence so-called through violent and, therefore, necessarily untruthful means we know only too painfully. Look at the daily destruction of property, life, and truth in the present war.

Complete Independence through truth and non-violence means the independence of every unit, 'be it the humblest of the nation, without distinction of race, colour or creed. This independence is never exclusive. It is, therefore, wholly compatible with interdependence within or without. Practice will always fall short of the theory, even as the drawn line falls short of the theoretical line of Euclid. Therefore, complete Independence will be complete only to the extent of our approach in practice to truth and non-violence.

Let the reader mentally plan out the whole of the constructive programme, and he will agree with me that, if it could be successfully worked out, the 'end of it would be the Independence we want. Has not Mr. Amery said that an agreement between the major parties, translated in my language, any agreement after communal unity which is only one item in the constructive programme, will be respected? We need not question his sincerity, for, if such unity is honestly, i.e. non-violently, attained, it will in itself contain the power to compel acceptance of the agreed demand.

On the other hand, there it is no such thing as an imaginary or even 'perfect definition of Independence through violence'. "For it presupposes only ascendancy of that party of the nation which makes the most effective use of violence. In it perfect equality, economic or otherwise, is inconceivable.

But for my purpose, which is to convince the reader of the necessity of following out the constructive programme in the non-violent effort, the acceptance of my argument about the ineffectiveness of violence for 'the attainment of independence is not required. The reader is welcome to the belief that Independence of the humblest unit is possible under the scheme of violence, if this effort enables him also to admit it is a certainty through the complete execution of the programme by the nation.

Let us now examine the items.

COMMUNAL UNITY

Everybody is agreed about the necessity of this unity. But everybody does not know that unity does not mean political unity which may be imposed. It means an unbreakable heart unity. The first thing essential for achieving such unity is for every Congressman, whatever his religion may be, to represent, in his own person Hindu, Muslim, Christian, Zoroastrian, Jew, etc., shortly, every Hindu and non-Hindu. He has to feel his identity with everyone of the millions of the inhabitants of Hindustan. In order to realise this, every Congressman will cultivate personal friendship with persons representing faiths other than his own. He should have the same regard for the other faiths as he has for his own.

In such a happy state of things. there would be no disgraceful cry at the stations such as "Hindu water" and "Muslim water" or "Hindu tea" and "Muslim tea". There would be no separate rooms or pots for Hindus and non-Hindus in schools and colleges, no communal schools, colleges and hospitals. The beginning of such a revolution has to be made by Congressmen without any political motive behind! the correct conduct. Political unity will be its natural fruit.

We have long been accustomed to think that power comes only through Legislative Assemblies, I have regarded this belief as a grave error brought about by inertia or hypnotism. A superficial study of British history has made us think that all power percolates to the people from parliaments. The truth is that power resides in the people and it is entrusted for the time being to those whom they may choose as their representatives. Parliaments have no power or even existence independently of the people. It has been my effort for the last twenty-one years to convince the people of this simple truth. Civil Disobedience is the storehouse of power. Imagine a whole people unwilling to conform to the laws of the legislative, and prepared to suffer the consequences of non-compliance! They will bring the whole legislative and executive machinery to a standstill. The police and the military are of us to coerce minorities however powerful they may be. But no police or military coercion can bend the resolute will of a people who are out for suffering to the uttermost.

And parliamentary procedure is good only when it's members are willing to conform to the will of the majority. In other words, it is fairly effective only among compatibles.

Here in India we have been pretending to work the parliamentary system under separate electorates which have created artificial incompatibles. Living unity can never come out of these artificial entities being brought together on a common platform. Such legislatures may function. But they can only be a platform for wrangling and sharing the crumbs of power that may fall from rulers whoever they may be. These rule with a rod of iron, and prevent the opposing elements from flying at one another's throats. I hold the emergence of complete Independence to be an impossibility out of such a disgrace.

Though I hold such strong views, I have come to the conclusion that so long as there are undesirable candidates for elective bodies. Congress should put up candidates in order to prevent reactionaries from entering such bodies.

REMOVAL OF UNTOUCHABILITY

At this time of the day it is unnecessary to dilate upon the necessity of the removal of this blot and curse upon Hinduism. Congressmen have certainly done much in this matter. But I am sorry to have to say that many Congressmen have looked upon this item as a mere political necessity and not something indispensable, so far as Hindus are concerned, for the very existence of Hinduism. If Hindu Congressmen take up the cause for its own sake, they will influence the so-called Sanatanis far more extensively than they have hitherto done. They should approach them not in a militant spirit but, as befits their non-violence, in a spirit of friendliness. And so far as the Harijans are concerned, every Hindu should make common cause with them and befriend them in their awful isolation-such isolation as perhaps the world has never seen in the monstrous immensity one witnesses in India. I know from experience how difficult the task is. But it is part of the task of building the edifice of *Swaraj*. And the road to *Swaraj* is steep and narrow. There are many slippery ascents and. many deep chasms. They have all to be negotiated with unfaltering step before we can reach the summit and breathe the fresh air of freedom.

PROHIBITION

Although like communal unity and removal of untouchability prohibition has been on the Congress programme since 1920, Congressmen have not taken the interest they might have taken in this very vital social and moral reform. If we are to reach our goal through non-violent effort, we may not leave to the future government the fate of lakhs of men and women who are labouring under the curse of intoxicants and narcotics.

Medical men can make a most effective contribution towards the removal of this evil. They have to discover ways of weaning the drunkard and the opium-addict from the curse.

Women and students have a special opportunity in advancing this reform. By many acts of loving service they can acquire on addicts a hold which will compel them to listen to the appeal to give up the evil habit.

Congress committees can open recreation booths where the tired labourer will rest his limbs, get healthy and cheap refreshments, find suitable games. All this work is fascinating and uplifting. The non-violent approach to *Swaraj* is a novel approach. In it old values give place to new. In the violent way such reforms may find no place. Believers in that way, in their impatience and, shall I say, ignorance, put off such things to the day of deliverance. They forget that lasting and healthy deliverance comes from within, i.e. from self-purification. Constructive workers make legal prohibition easy and successful even if they do not pave the way for it.

KHADI

Khadi is a controversial subject. Many people think that in advocating *khadi* I am sailing against a headwind and am sure to sink the ship of *Swaraj* and that I am taking the country to the dark ages. I do not propose to argue the case for *khadi* in this brief survey. I have argued. It sufficiently elsewhere. Here I want to show what every Congressman, and for that matter every Indian, can do to advance the cause of *khadi*. It connotes the beginning of economic freedom arid equality of all in the country. "The proof of the pudding is in the eating." Let everyone try, and he or she will find out for himself or herself the truth of what I am saying. *Khadi* must be taken with all its implications. It means a wholesale Swadeshi mentality, a determination to find all the necessaries of life in India and that too through the labour and intellect of the villagers. That means a reversal of the existing process. That is to say that, instead of half a dozen cities of India and Great Britain living on the exploitation and the ruin of the 7,00,000 villages of India, the latter will be largely self-contained, and will voluntarily serve the cities of India and even the outside world in so far as it benefits both the parties.

This needs a revolutionary change in the mentality and tastes of many. Easy though the non-violent way is in many respects, it is very difficult in many others. It vitally touches the life of every single Indian, makes him feel aglow with the possession of a power that has lain hidden within himself, and makes him proud of his identity with every drop of the ocean of Indian humanity. This non-violence is not the inanity for which we have mistaken it through all these long ages; it is the most potent force as yet known to mankind and on which its very existence is dependent. It is that force which I have tried to present to the Congress and through it to the world. *Khadi* to me is the symbol of unity of Indian humanity, of its economic freedom and equality and, therefore, ultimately, in the poetic expression of Jawaharlal Nehru, "the livery of India's freedom".

Moreover, *khadi* mentality means decentralisation of the production and distribution of the 'necessaries of life. Therefore, the formula so far evolved is, every village to produce all its necessaries and a certain percentage in addition for the requirements of the cities.

Heavy industries will need be centralised and nationalised. But they will occupy the least pans of the vast national activity which will mainly be in the villages.

Having explained the implications of khadi, I must indicate what Congressmen can and should do towards its promotion. Production of *khadi* includes cotton growing, picking, ginning, cleaning, carding, slivering, spinning, sizing, dyeing, preparing the warp and the woof, weaving, and washing. These, with the exception of dyeing, are essential processes. Every one of them can be effectively handled in the villages and is being so handled in many villages throughout India which the A.I.S.A is covering. According to the latest report the following are the interesting figures:

2,75,146 villagers, including 19,645 Harijans and 57,378 Muslims, scattered in at least 13,451 villages, received, as spinners, weavers, etc., Rs. 34,85,609 in 1940. The spinners were largely women.

Yet the work done is only one-hundredth part of what could be done if Congressmen honestly took up the *khadi* programme. Since the wanton destruction of this central village industry and the allied handicrafts, intelligence and brightness have fled from the villages, leaving them inane, lustreless, and reduced almost to the state of their ill-kept cattle.

If Congressmen will be true to their Congress call in respect of *khadi,* they will carry out the instructions of the A I.S.A issued from time to time as to the part they can play in *khadi* planning. Only a few broad rules can be laid down here:

1. Every family with a plot of ground can grow cotton at least for family use. Cotton growing is easy process. In Bihar the cultivators were by law compelled to grow indigo on 3/20 of their cultivable land. This was in the interest of the foreign indigo planter. Why cannot we grow cotton voluntarily for the nation on a certain portion of our land? The reader will note that decentralisation commences from the beginning of the *khadi* processes. Today cotton crop is centralised and has to be sent to distant parts of India. Before the war it used to be sent principally to Britain and Japan. It was and still is a money crop and, therefore, subject to the fluctuations of the market. Under the khadi scheme cotton-growing becomes free from this uncertainty and gamble. The grower grows what he needs. The farmer needs to know that his first business is to grow for his my need. When he does that, he will reduce the chance of a low market ruining him.
2. Every spinner would buy-if he has not his own-enough

cotton for ginning, which he can easily do without the hand-ginning roller frame. He can gin his own portion with a board and an iron rolling pin. Where this is considered impractical hand ginned cotton should be bought and carded. Carding for self can be done well on a tiny bow without much effort. The greater the decentralisation of labour, the simpler and cheaper the tools. The slivers made, the process of spinning commences. I strongly recommend the dhanush takli. I have used it frequently. My speed on it is almost the same as on the wheel. I draw a finer thread and the strength and evenness of the yarn are greater on the dhanush takli than on the wheel. This may not, however, hold good for all. My emphasis on the dhanush takli is based on the fact that it is more easily made, is cheaper than and does not require frequent repairs like the wheel. Unless one knows how to make the two mats and to adjust them when they slip or to put the wheel right when it refuses to work, the wheel has often to lie idle. Moreover, if the millions take to spinning at once, as they well may have to, the dhanush takli, being the instrument most easily made and handled, is the only tool that can meet the demand. It is more easily made even than the simple takli. The best, easiest and cheapest way is to make it oneself. Indeed one ought to learn how to handle and make simple tools. Imagine the unifying and educative effect of the whole nation simultaneously taking part in the processes up to spinning! Consider the leveling effect of the bond of common labour between the rich and the poor!

Yarn thus produced may be used in three ways: by presenting it to the A.I.S.A. for the sake of the poor, by having it woven for personal use, or by getting as much *khadi* for it as it can buy. It is clear enough that the finer and better the yarn the greater will be its value. If Congressmen will put their heart into the work, they will make improvements in the tools and make many discoveries. In our ,country there has been a divorce between labour and intelligence. The result has been stagnation. If there is an indissoluble marriage between the two, and that in the manner here suggested, the resultant good will be inestimable.

In this scheme of nation-wide spinning as a sacrifice, I do not expect the average man or woman to give more than one hour daily to this.

OTHER VILLAGE INDUSTRIES

These stand on a different footing from *khadi:* There is not much scope for voluntary labour in them. Each industry will take the labour of only a certain number of hands. These industries come in as a hand-maid to *khadi*. They cannot exist without *khadi,* and *khadi* will be robbed of its dignity without them. Village economy cannot be complete without the essential village industries such as hand-grinding, hand-pounding, soap-making, paper-making, match-making, tanning, oil-pressing, etc. Congressmen can interest themselves in these and if they are villagers or will settle down in villages, they will give these industries a new life and a new dress. All should make it a point of honour to use only village articles whenever and wherever available. Given the demand there is no doubt that most of our wants can be supplied from our villages. When we have become village-minded, we will not want imitations of the West or machine-made products, but we will develop a true national taste in keeping with the vision of a new India in which pauperism, starvation and idleness will be unknown.

VILLAGE SANITATION

Divorce between intelligence and labour has resulted in criminal negligence of the villages. And so, instead of having graceful hamlets dotting the land, we have dung-heaps. The approach to many villages is not a refreshing experience. Often one would like to shut one's eyes and stuff one's nose; such is the surrounding dirt and offending smell. If the majority of Congressmen were derived from our villages, as they should be, they should be able to make our villages models of cleanliness in every sense of the word. But they have never considered it their duty to identify themselves with the villagers in their daily lives. A sense of national or social sanitation is not a virtue among us. We may take a kind of a bath, but we do not mind dirtying the well or the tank or the river by whose side or in which we perform ablutions. I regard this defect as a great vice which is responsible for the disgraceful state of our villages and the sacred banks of the sacred rivers and for the diseases that spring from insanitation.

NEW OR BASIC EDUCATION

This is a new subject. But the members of the Working Committee felt so much interested in it that they gave a charter to the organisers of the Hindustani Talimi Sangh which has been functioning since the Haripura session. This is a big field of work for many Congressmen. This education is meant to transform village children into model villagers. It is principally designed for them. The inspiration for it has come from the villages. Congressmen who want to build up the structure of *Swaraj* from its very foundation dare not neglect the children. Foreign rule has unconsciously, though none the less surely, begun with the children in the field of education. Primary education is a farce designed without regard to the wants of the India of the villages and for that Ipatter even of the cities. Basic education links the children, whether of the cities or the villages, to all that is best and lasting in India. It develops both the body and the mind, and keeps the child rooted to the soil with a glorious vision of the future in the realisation of which he or she begins to take his or her share from the very commencement of his or her career in school. Congressmen would find it of absorbing interest benefiting themselves equally with the children with whom they come in contact: Let those who wish, put themselves in touch with the Secretary of the Sangh at Sevagram.

ADULT EDUCATION

This has been woefully neglected by Congressmen. Where they have not neglected it, they have been satisfied with teaching illiterates to read and write. If I had charge of adult education, I should begin with opening the minds of the adult pupils to the greatness and vastness of their country. The villager's India is contained in his village. If he goes to another village, he talks of his own village as his home. Hindustan is for him a geographical term. We have no notion I of the ignorance prevailing in the villages. The villagers know nothing of foreign rule and its evils. What little knowledge they have picked up fills them with the awe the foreigner inspires. The result is the dread and hatred of the foreigner and his rule. They do not know how to get rid of it. They do not know that the foreigner's presence is due to their own weaknesses and their ignorance of the power they possess to rid themselves of the foreign rule. My adult education means, therefore, first, true political education of the adult by word of mouth. Seeing that this will be mapped out, it can be given without fear. I imagine that it is too late in the day for authority to interfere with this type of education; but if there is interference, there must be a fight for this elementary right without which there can be no *Swaraj*. Of course, in all I have written, openness has been assumed. Non-violence abhors fear and, therefore, secrecy. Side by side with the education by the mouth will be the literary education. This is itself a speciality. Many methods are being tried in order to shorten the period of education. A temporary or permanent board of experts may be appointed by the Working Committee to give shape to the idea here adumbrat'1d and guide the workers. I admit that what I have said in this paragraph only points the way but does not tell the average Congressman how to go about it. Nor is every Congressman fitted for this highly special work. But Congressmen who are teachers should find no difficulty in laying down a course in keeping with the suggestions made herein.

WOMEN

I have included service of women in the constructive programme, for though *Satyagraha* has automatically brought India's women out from their darkness, as nothing else could have in such an incredibly short space of time, Congressmen have not felt the call to see that women became equal partners in the fight for *Swaraj.* They have not realised that woman must be the true helpmate of man in the mission of service. Woman has been suppressed under custom and law for which man was responsible and in the shaping of which she had no hand. In a plan of life based on non-violence, woman has as much right to shape her own destiny as man has to shape his. But as every right in a non-violent society proceeds from the previous performance of a duty, it follows that rules of social conduct must be framed by mutual cooperation and consultation. They can never be imposed from outside. Men have not realised this truth in its fullness in their behaviour towards women. They have considered themselves to be lords and masters of women instead of considering them as their friends and co-workers. It is the privilege of Congressmen to give the women of India a lifting hand. Women are in the position somewhat of the slave of old who did not know that he could or ever had to be free. And when freedom came, for the moment he felt helpless. Women have been taught to regard themselves as slaves of men. It is up to Congressmen to see that they enable them to realise their full status and play their part as equals of men.

This revolution is easy, if the mind is made up. Let Congressmen begin with their own homes. Wives should not be dolls and objects of indulgence, but should be treated as honoured comrades in common service. To this end those who have not received a liberal education should receive such instruction as is possible from their husbands. The same observation applies, with the necessary changes, to mothers and daughters.

It is hardly necessary to point out that I have given a one-sided picture of the helpless state of India's women. I am quite conscious of the fact that in the villages generally they hold their own with their menfolk and in some respects even rule them. But to the impartial outsider the legal and customary status of woman is bad enough throughout and demands radical alteration.

EDUCATION IN HEALTH AND HYGIENE

Having given a place to village sanitation, the question may be asked why give a separate place to education in health and hygiene? It might have been bracketed with sanitation, but I did not wish to interfere with the items. Mention of mere sanitation is not enough to include health and hygiene. The art of keeping one's health and the knowledge of hygiene is by itself a separate subject of study and corresponding practice. In a well-ordered society the citizens know and observe the laws of health and hygiene. It is established beyond doubt that ignorance and neglect of the laws of health and hygiene are responsible for the majority of diseases to which mankind is heir. The very high death rate among us is no doubt due largely to our gnawing poverty, but it could be mitigated if the people were properly educated about health and hygiene.

Mens sana in corpore sana is perhaps the first law for humanity. A healthy mind in a healthy body is self-evident truth. There is an inevitable connection between mind and body. If we were in possession of healthy minds, we would shed all violence and, naturally obeying the laws of health, we would have healthy bodies without an effort. I hope, therefore, that no Congressman will disregard this item of the constructive programme. The fundamental laws of health and hygiene are simple and easily learnt. The difficulty is about their observance. Here are some:

Think the purest thoughts and banish all idle and impure thoughts.

Breathe the freshest air day and night.

Establish a balance between bodily and mental work.

Stand erect, sit erect, and be neat and clean in everyone of your acts, and let these be an expression of your inner condition.

Eat to live for service of fellow-men. Do not live for indulging yourselves. Hence your food must be just enough to keep your mind and body in good order. Man becomes what he eats.

Your water, food and air must be clean, and you will not be satisfied with mere personal cleanliness, but you will infect your surroundings with the same three-fold cleanliness that you will desire for yourselves.

PROVINCIAL LANGUAGES

Our love of the English language in preference to our own mother tongue has caused a deep chasm between the educated and politically-minded classes and the masses. The languages of India have suffered impoverishment. We flounder when we make the vain attempt to express abstruse thought in the mother tongue. There are no equivalents for scientific terms. The result has been disastrous. The masses remain cut off from the modern mind. We are too near our own times correctly to measure the disservice caused to India by this neglect of its great languages. It is easy enough to understand that, unless we undo the mischief, the mass mind must remain imprisoned. The masses can make no solid contribution to the construction of Swaraj. It is inherent in Swaraj based on non-violence that every individual makes his own direct contribution to the Independence movement. The masses cannot do this fully unless they understand every step with all its implications. This is impossible unless every step is explained in their own languages.

NATIONAL LANGUAGE

And then for all-India intercourse we need, from among the Indian stock, a language which the largest number of people already know and understand and which the others can easily pick up. This language is indisputably Hindi. It is spoken and understood by both Hindus and Muslims of the North. It is called Urdu when it is written in the Urdu character. The Congress, in its famous resolution passed at the Cawnpore session in 1925, called this all-India speech Hindustani. And since that time, in theory at least, Hindustani has been the Rashtra Bhasha. I say 'in theory' because even Congressmen have not practised it as they should have. In 1920 adeliberate attempt was begun to recognise the importance of Indian languages for the political education of the masses, as also of an all-India common speech which politically-minded India could easily speak and which Congressmen from the different provinces could understand at all-India gatherings of the Congress. Such National language should enable one to understand and speak both forms of speech and write in both the scripts.

I am sorry to have to say that many Congressmen have failed to carry out that resolution. And so we have, in my opinion, the shameful spectacle of Congressmen insisting on speaking in English and compelling others to do likewise for their sakes. The spell that English has cast on us is not yet broken. Being under it, we are impeding the progress of India towards her goal. Our love of the masses must be skin-deep, if we will not take the trouble of spending over learning Hindustani" as many months as the years we spend over learning English.

ECONOMIC EQUALITY

This last is the master key to non-violent Independence. Working for economic equality means abolishing the eternal conflict between capital and labour. It means the leveling down of the few rich in whose hands is concentrated the bulk of the nation's wealth on the one hand, and the leveling up of the semi-starved naked millions on the other. A non-violent system of government is clearly an impossibility so-long as the wide gulf between the rich and the hungry millions persists. The contrast between the palaces of New Delhi and the miserable hovels of the poor labouring class nearby cannot last one day in a free India in which the poor will enjoy the same power as the richest in the land. A violent and bloody revolution is a certainty one day unless there is a voluntary abdication of riches and the power that riches give and sharing them for the common good.

I adhere to my doctrine of trusteeship in spite of the ridicule that has been poured upon it. It is true that it is difficult to reach. So is non-violence. But we made up our minds in 1920 to negotiate that steep ascent. We have found it worth the effort. It involves a daily growing appreciation of the working of non-violence. It is expected that Congressmen will make a diligent search and reason out for themselves the why and the wherefore of non-violence. They should ask themselves how the existing inequalities can be abolished violently or non-violently. I think we know the violent way. It has not succeeded anywhere.

This non-violent experiment is still in the making. We have nothing much yet to show by way of demonstration. It is certain, however, that the method has begun to work though ever so slowly in the direction of equality. And since non-violence is a process of conversion, the conversion, if achieved, must be permanent. A society or a nation constructed non-violently must be able to, withstand attack upon its structure from without or within. We have moneyed Congressmen in the organization. They have to lead the way. This fight provides an opportunity for the closest heart-searching on the part of every individual Congressman. If ever we are to achieve equality, the foundation has to be laid now. Those who think that the major reforms will come after the advent of *Swaraj* are deceiving themselves as to the elementary working of non-violent *Swaraj*. It will not drop from heaven all of a sudden one fine morning. But it has to be built up brick by brick by corporate self-effort. We have traveled a fair way in that direction. But a much longer and weary distance has to be covered before we can behold *Swaraj* in its glorious majesty. Every Congressman has to ask himself what he has done towards the attainment of economic equality.

KISANS

The programme is not exhaustive. *Swaraj* is a mighty structure. Eighty crores of hands have to work at building it. Of these kisans, i.e., the peasantry are the largest part. In fact, being the bulk of them (probably over 80%) the kisans should be the Congress. But they are not. When they become conscious of their non-violent strength, no power on earth can resist them.

They must not be used for power politics. I consider it to be contrary to the non-violent method. Those who would know my methods of organising kisans may profitably study the movement in Champaran when *Satyagraha* was tried for the first time in India with the result all India knows. It became a mass movement which remained wholly non-violent from start to finish. It affected over twenty lakhs of kisans. The struggle centered round one specific grievance which was" century old. There had been several violent revolts to get rid of the grievance. The kisans were suppressed. The non-violent remedy succeeded in full in six months. The kisans of Champaran became politically conscious without any direct effort. The tangible proof they had of the working of non-violence to remove their grievance drew them to the Congress, and led by Babu Brijkishoreprasad and Babu Rajendra Prasad they gave a good account of themselves during the past Civil Disobedience campaigns.

The reader may also profitably study the kisan movements in Kheda, Bardoli and Borsad. The secret of success lies in a refusal to exploit the kisans. for political purposes outside their own personal and felt grievances. Organisation round a specific wrong they understand. They need no sermons on non-violence. Let them learn to apply non-violence as an effective remedy which they can understand, and later when they are told that the method they were applying was non-violent, they readily recognise it as such.

From these illustrations Congressmen who care could study how work can be done for and among kisans. I hold that the method that some Congressmen have followed to organise kisans has done them no good and has probably harmed them. Anyway they have not used the non-violent method. Be it said to the credit of some of these workers that they frankly admit that they do not believe in the non-violent. method. My advice to such workers would be that they should neither use the Congress name nor work as Congressmen.

The reader will now understand why I have refrained from the competition to organise kisans and Labour on an all-

India basis. How I wish that all hands pulled in the same direction! But perhaps in a huge country like ours it is impossible. Anyway, in non-violence there is no coercion. Cold reason and demonstration of the working of non-violence must be trusted to do the work. In my opinion, like labour, they should have under the Congress, a department working for their specific questions.

LABOUR

Ahmedabad Labour Union is a model for all India to copy. Its basis is non-violence, pure and simple. It has never had a set-back in its career. It has gone on from strength to strength without fuss and without show. It has its hospital, its schools for the children of the mill-hands, its classes for adults, its own printing press and *khadi* depot, and its own residential quarters. Almost all the hands are voters and decide the fate of elections. They came on the voters' list at the instance of the Provincial Congress Committee. The organisation has never taken part in party politics of the Congress. It influences the municipal policy of the city. It has to its credit very successful strikes which were wholly non-violent (Mill owners and labour have governed their relations largely through voluntary arbitration. If I had my way, I would-regulate all the labour organisations of India after the Ahmedabad model. It has never sought to intrude itself upon the all-India Trade Union Congress and has been uninfluenced by that Congress. A time; I hope, will come when it will be possible for the Trade Union Congress to accept the Ahmedabad method and have the Ahmedabad organization as part of the All-India Union. But I am in no hurry. It will come in its, own time.'

ADIVASIS

The term adivasi, like raniparaj, is a coined word. Raniparaj stands for kaliparaj (meaning black people, though their skin is no more black than that of any other). It was coined, I think by Shri Jugatram. The term adivasi (for Bhils, Gonds, or others variously described as Hill Tribes or aboriginals) means literally original inhabitants and was coined, I believe, by Thakkar Bapa.

Service of adivasi is also a part of the constructive programme. Though they are the sixteenth number in this programme, they are not the least in point of importance. Our country is so vast and the races so varied that the best of us cannot know all there is to know of men and their condition. As one discovers this for oneself, one realises how difficult it is to make good our claim: to be one nation, unless every unit has a living consciousness of. being one with every other.

The advasi are over two crores in all India. Bapa began work among the Bhils years ago in Gujarat. In about 1940, Shri Balasaheb Kher threw himself with his usual zeal into this much-needed service in the Thana District. He is now President of the 'Adivasi Seva MandaI.'

There are several such other workers in other parts of India and yet they are too few. Truly, "the harvest is rich but the labourers are few." Who can deny that all such service is not merely' humanitarian but solidly national, and brings us nearer to true independence?

LEPERS

Leper is a word of bad odour. India is perhaps a home of lepers next only to Central Africa. Yet they are as much a part of society as the tallest among us. But the tall absorb our attention though they are least in need of it. The lot of the lepers who are much in need of attention is studied neglect. I am tempted to call it heartless, which it certainly is, in terms of non-violence. It is, largely the missionary who, be it said to his credit, bestows care on him. The only institution run by an Indian, as a pure labour of love, is by Shri Manohar Diwan near Wardha. It is working under the inspiration and guidance of Shri Vinoba Bhave. If India was pulsating with new life, if we were all in earnest about winning independence in the quickest manner possible by truthful and non-violent means, there would not be a leper or beggar in India uncared for and unaccounted for. In this revised edition I am deliberately introducing the leper as a link in the chain of constructive effort. For, what the leper is in India, that we are,. if we will but look about us, or the modern civilised world. Examine the condition of our brethren across the ocean and the truth of my remark will be borne home to us.

STUDENTS

I have reserved students to the last. I have always cultivated close contact with them. They know me and I know them. They have given me service. Many ex-collegians are my esteemed co-workers, I know that they are the hope of the future. In the heyday of non-cooperation they were invited to leave their schools and colleges. Some professors and students who responded to the congress call have remained steadfast and gained much for the country and themselves. The call has not been repeated for there is not the atmosphere for it. But experience has shown that the lure of the current education, though it is false and unnatural, is too much for the youth of the country. College education provides a career. It is a passport for entrance to the charmed circle. Pardonable hunger for knowledge cannot be satisfied otherwise than by going through the usual rut. They do not mind the waste of precious years in acquiring knowledge of an utterly foreign language which takes the place of the mother tongue. The sin of it is never felt. They and their teachers have made up their minds that the indigenous languages are useless for gaining access to modern thought and the modern sciences. I wonder how the Japanese are faring. For, their education, I understand, is all given in Japanese. The Chinese General- issimo knows very little, if anything, of English.

But such as the students are, it is from these young men and women that the future leaders of the nation are to rise. Unfortunately they are acted upon, by every variety of influence Non-violence offers them little attraction. A blow for a blow or two. Of one is an easily understandable proposition. It seems to yield immediate result though momentary. It is a never-ending trial of brute strength as we see in time of war among brutes or among human beings. Appreciation of non-violence means patient research and still more patient and difficult practice. I have not entered the list of competitors for the students' hand, for the reasons that have dictated my course about Kisans and Labour. But I am myself a fellow student, using the word in its broader sense. My university is different from theirs. They have a standing invitation from me to come to my university and join me in my search. Here are the terms:

1. Students must not take part in party politics. They are students, searchers; not politicians.
2. They may not resort to political strikes. They must have their heroes, but their devotion to them is to be shown by copying the best in their heroes, not by going on strikes, if the heroes are imprisoned or die or are even sent to the gallows. If their grief is unbearable and if all the students feel equally, schools or colleges may be closed on such occasions, with the consent of their principals. If the principals will not listen, it is open to the students to leave their institutions in becoming manner till the managers repent and recall them. On no account may they use coercion against dissentients or against the authorities. They must have the confidence that, if they are united and dignified. in their conduct, they are sure to win.
3. They must all do sacrificial spinning in a scientific manner. Their tools shall be always neat, clean, and in good order and condition. If possible, they will learn to make them themselves. Their yarn will naturally be of the highest quality. They will study the literature about spinning with all its economic, social, moral and political implications. . .
4. They will be khadi-users all through and use village products to the exclusion of all analogous things, foreign or machine-made.
5. They may not impose Vande Mataram or the National Flag on others. "They may wear National Flag buttons on their own persons but not force others to do the same.
6. They can enforce the message of the tricolour nag in their own persons and harbour neither communalism

nor untouchability in their hearts. They will cultivate real friendship with students of other faiths and with Harijans as if they were their own kith and kin.'

7. They will make it a point to give first aid to their injured neighbours and do scavenging and cleaning in the neighbouring villages and instruct village children and adults.
8. They will learn the national language, Hindustani, its present double dress, two forms of speech and two scripts, so that they may feel at home whether Hindi, Urdu is spoken and nagari or urdu script is written.
9. They will translate into their own mother tongue every thing new they may learn, and transmit it in their weekly rounds to the surrounding villages.'
10. They will do nothing in secret, they will be above board in all their dealings, they will lead a pure life of self-restraint shed an fear and be always ready to protect their weak fellow-students, and ready to quell riots by non-violent conduct at the risk of their lives. And when the final heat of the struggle comes they will leave their institutions and, if need be sacrifice themselves for the freedom of their country.
11. They will be scrupulously correct and chivalrous in their behaviour towards their girl fellow-students.

For working out the programme I have sketched for them the students must find time. I know that they waste a great deal of time in idleness. By strict economy, they can save many hours. But I do not want to put an undue strain upon any student. I would therefore, advise patriotic students to lose one year, not at a stretch but spread it over their whole study. They will find that one year so given will not be a waste of time. The effort will add to their equipment, mental, moral and physical, and they will have made even during their studies it substantial contribution to the freedom movement.

PLACE OF CIVIL DISOBEDIENCE

I have said in these pages that Civil Disobedience is not absolutely necessary to win freedom through purely non-violent effort, if the cooperation of the whole nation is secured in the constructive programme. But such good luck rarely favours nations or individuals. Therefore, it is necessary to know the place of Civil Disobedience in a nation-wide non-violent effort it has three definite functions:

1. It can be effectively offered for the redress of local wrong.
2. It can be offered without regard to effect, though aimed at a particular wrong or evil, by way of self-immolation in order to rouse local consciousness or conscience. Such was the case in Champaran when I offered Civil Disobedience without any regard to the effect and well knowing that even the people might remain apathetic. That it proved otherwise may be taken, according to taste, as God's grace or a stroke of good luck.
3. In the place of full response to constructive effort, it can be offered as it was in 1941. Though it was a contribution to and part of the battle for freedom, it was purposely centered round a particular issue, i.e. free speech. Civil Disobedience can never be directed for a general cause such as for Independence. The issue must be definite and capable of being clearly understood and within the power; of the opponent to yield. This method properly applied must lead to the final goal.

I have not examined here the full scope and possibilities of Civil Disobedience. I have touched enough of it to enable the reader to understand the connection between the constructive programme and Civil Disobedience. In the first two cases, no elaborate constructive programme was or could be necessary. But when Civil Disobedience is itself devised for the attainment of Independence, previous preparation is necessary, and it has to be backed by the visible and conscious effort of those who are engaged in the battle. Civil Disobedience is thus a stimulation for the fighters and a challenge to the opponent. It should be clear to the reader that Civil Disobedience in terms of Independence without the cooperation of the millions by way of constructive effort is mere bravado and worse than useless.

CONCLUSION

This is not a thesis written on behalf of the Congress or at the instance of the Central Office. It is the outcome of conversations I had with some co-workers in Sevagram. They had felt the want of something from my pen showing the connection between constructive programme and Civil Disobedience and how the former might be worked. I have endeavoured to supply the want in this pamphlet. It does not purport to be exhaustive, but it is sufficiently indicative of the way the programme should be worked.

Let not the reader make the mistake of laughing at any of the items as being part of the movement for Independence. Many people do many things, big and small, without connecting them with non-violence or Independence. They have then their limited value as expected. The same man appearing as a civilian may be of no consequence, but appearing in his capacity as General he is a big personage, holding the lives of millions at his mercy. Similarly, the charkha in the hands of a poor widow brings a paltry pice to her I in the hands of Jawaharlal it is an instrument of India's freedom. It is the office which gives the charkha its dignity. It is the office assigned to the constructive programme which gives it an irresistible prestige and power. .

Such at least is my view. It may be that of a mad man. If it makes no appeal to the Congressman, I must be rejected. For my handling of Civil Disobedience without the constructive programme will be like a paralysed hand attempting to lift a spoon.

Poona, U3-11-1945

M K Gandhi

Quenstion Bank on 'Reading Gandhi'

Note: Three questions in all have to be attempted. One question from ***Section I*** *is compulsory. Maximum marks: 38. 12 marks for internal assessment.*

Section – I (14 marks)

1. Define 'text'. What are the different ways of reading a text? Differentiate between the 'textual' and 'contextual' ways of reading a text.
2. Elaborate the differences between textual and contextual approached to reading a text. (2006)
3. Discuss the various strategies of interpreting a text given by Terence Ball.
4. Discuss Quentin Skinner's approach to the study of classics.
5. Analyze the mythology of doctrine given by Quentin Skinner.
6. Discuss the methodologies to read a text according to Quentin Skinner. (2005)
7. Comment and contrast between Western and Indian writings on *Hind Swaraj*. (2006)
8. What is a classic? Do you think *Hind Swaraj* is a classic? Give reasons for your answer.
9. Discuss the various ways of reading a classic. Does *Hind Swaraj* qualify as a classic? (2005)
10. To what extent do you think Gandhi was a postmodernist thinker? Give arguments in favour of your answer. (April, 2008)

Section – II (12 marks)

1. Discuss Gandhi's concept of *swaraj.*
2. Discuss the socio-historical context in which *Hind Swaraj* was written.
3. Discuss Gandhi's critique of modern civilization as given in *Hind Swaraj.*
4. Analyse the 'condition of India' as discussed in *Hind Swaraj.*
5. Describe in detail the concept of "passive resistance" as discussed in *Hind Swaraj.*
6. What message does Gandhi wish to convey to the western word through *Hind Swaraj*?(2005)
7. How does Gandhi analyse the condition of India in *Hind Swaraj*? (2006)

Section – III (12 marks)

1. Discuss Anthony J Parel's analysis of *Hind Swaraj.*
2. On the basis of discussion by Anthony Parel, discuss the impact of *Hind Swaraj* on Indian intelligentsia.
3. Discuss Bhikhu Parekh's views on Gandhi's concept of Satyagraha.
4. What is Satyagraha? Discuss its basic postulates and contemporary relevance. (2005)
5. Discuss Bhikhu Parekh's views on Gandhi's critique of modernity.
6. Discuss David Hardiman's views on Gandhi's "alternative modernity".
7. Discuss the reasons why Hardiman considers Gandhi as a modern thinker.

Section – IV (12marks)

1. Critically examine Gandhi's concept of nationalism.
2. What is nationalism? Discuss Gandhi's views on nationalism in the context of modern India. (2005)
3. Examine Gandhi's views on communal unity in today's context.
4. Examine Gandhi's views on the women's question.

5. Discuss Gandhi's stand on the question of equality of women.
6. Why does Gandhi consider untouchability as the greatest curse of Hinduism? Discuss.
7. Do you agree with the statement that the ecological problems of the modern world have a lot of Gandhian solutions? (April, 2008)
8. Discuss the relevance of Gandhian thought in modern times.
9. Discuss the social and political thought of Gandhi.

Sample of Project and Assignment for Internal Assessment

I. Project

(*as part of internal assessment; maximum marks: 25*)

Visit any one of the following places and prepare a Report of your visit.

(*a*) Gandhi Smriti, Tees January Marg, New Delhi.
(*b*) Gandhi Darshan, Near Rajghat, New Delhi.
(*c*) Gandhi Museum and Library, Opposite Rajghat, New Delhi.

The report should be of at least 3000 words, neatly written or typed in A-4 size sheets and should have the following information:

- The significance of the place.
- The salient features of the place, its location, layout and significant items on display.
- Information regarding its management and administration.
- Interview with an important official/employee of the place or visitor.
- Personal impressions of the place.

II. Assignment

(*as part of internal assessment; maximum marks: 25*)

Topic: Close Reading of *Hind Swaraj*

Prepare a summary of the main ideas mentioned by Gandhi in *Hind Swaraj* touching upon the following points:

- What was the immediate reason for Gandhi to write *Hind Swaraj* ?
- When was it written and where?
- Structure of the Book (dialogue; number of chapters; historical and philosophical division)
- Gandhi's arguments on the following issues:

1. Contribution of Moderates; need for new approach: use of soul force—Chapters I, II and III
2. *Swaraj* does not mean indiscriminate imitation of the English.—Chapter IV, V (Views on British Parliament, Prime Minister and Press).
3. Gandhi's idea of 'modern civilisation'—Chapter-VI
4. Reasons why India lost to England—Chapter-VII, Irreligious nature of civilisation—Chapter-VIII; its spell-binding nature—Chapter-VIII; Agents: Railways— also how Gandhi describes India as one nation—Chapter-IX; Communal distrust and Hindu-Muslim question: Chapter-X; Lawyers: Chapter-XI; Doctors: Chapter-XII
5. True civilisation is Indian civilisation : Chapter-XIII
6. India can achieve *swaraj* by following Indian civilisation: Chapter—XIV; violence is not a feature of Indian civilisation: example of Italy not to be followed-Chapter-XV; importance of ends and means—Chapter-XVI; India can win independence through 'passive resistance'—Chapter-XVII; importance of education - Chapter-XVIII; machinery should not make humans lose jobs—Chapter-XIX
7. Gandhi's definition of *swaraj* and its prerequisites.

The Syllabus

Course Name: **Reading Gandhi**
Interdisciplinary Concurrent Course for students of BA (Hons) I year
Maximum Marks:50

The course seeks to meet two essential objectives: one to acquaint the students with the art of reading texts, to enable students to grasp its conceptual and argumentative structure and to help them acquire the skills to locate the texts in the broader intellectual and socio-historical context. Two, it aims to acquaint the students with the social and political thought of Gandhi. We focus on Gandhi for three reasons: first, Gandhi is highly original; second, some of his texts have the requisite argumentative structure; third, the availability of a wide range of critical commentaries on his work. The themes in Gandhian thought that are chosen for a close reading are particularly relevant for our times.

1. Ways to read a text: textual and contextual.

Readings: Terence Ball, *Reappraising Political Theory,* Chapter I, OUP, 1995.

Quentin Skinner, "Meaning and Understanding in the History of Ideas", in *Visions of Politics,* Volume I, CUP, Cambridge, 2002.

2. Gandhi in his own words: A close reading of *Hind Swaraj.*

3. Commentaries on *Hind Swaraj* and Gandhian thought.

Readings:

(a) "Introduction", MK Gandhi, *Hind Swaraj and other Writings,* (ed) AJ Parel, 1997.
(b) B Parekh, *Gandhi,* 1997, Chapter IV("Satyagraha") and Chapter V ("The Critique of Modernity");
(c) D Hardiman, *Gandhi in His Times and Ours,* 2003, Chapter IV ("An Alternative Modernity")

4. Gandhi and Modern India

(a) Nationalism
(b) Communal Unity
(c) Women's Question
(d) Untouchability

Readings: this component will contain the following selections from Gandhi's *India of My Dreams* (Compiled by RK Prabhu)

(a) "The Meaning of Swaraj"(No.2)
(b) "In Defence of Nationalism" (No.3)
(c) "India's Cultural Heritage" (No.45)
(d) "Regeneration of Indian Women" (No.54)
(e) "Women's Education" (No.55)
(f) "Communal Unity" (No.59)
(g) "The Curse of Untouchability"(No.61)
(h) "Religious Tolerance in India" (No.62)
(i) "The Problem of Minorities" (No.66)

Bibliography

Primary Sources for the Course on 'Reading Gandhi':

Writings by MK Gandhi

Relevant sections of *Collected Works of Mahatma Gandhi,* Hundred Volumes, Publications Division, Ministry of Information and Broadcasting, Government of India, New Delhi, 1958–83(Vol.XCVIII contains the Subject Index to the other volumes and is helpful in searching material according to the topic one wants to study)

Gandhi, M.K.,*Story of My Experiments With Truth,* Vol.I translated by Mahadev Desai from Gujarati; Vol.II translated by Mahadev Desai and Pyarelal Nair (*incorrect spelling of Nayyar)* from Gujarati, Navajivan Press, Ahmedabad, 1927-29.

Gandhi, Mohandas K.,*Hind Swaraj or Indian Home Rule,* Navajivan Publishing House, Ahmedabad, 1931.

Gandhi, M.K., *Ethical Religion: Neethi Dharma* Translated by A Rama Iyer from Hindi.,S Ganesan, Madras, 1930.

Gandhi, M.K., *Satyagraha in South Africa,* Navajivan Publishing House, Ahmedabad, 1975.

Gandhi, M.K., *Constructive Programme: Its Meaning and Place,* Navajivan Publishing House, Ahmedabad, Revised and enlarged edition, 1945.

Gandhi, M.K., *The Bhagwadgita,* Orient Paperbacks, Delhi, 1998.

Gandhi, M.K., *Delhi Diary,* (Prayer Speeches from 10-947 to 30-1-48) Navajivan Publishing House, Ahmedabad, 1948(written in third person and corrected by Gandhi till the last speech before his death)

Primary Sources: As prescribed for this paper by Delhi University:

Ball, Terence, *Reappraising Political Theory,* Chapter I, OUP, 1995.

Hardiman, D., Chapter IV, 'An Alternative Modernity', *Gandhi in His Times and Ours,* 2003.

Gandhi, MK., *India of My Dreams* (Compiled by RK Prabhu), 'The Meaning of Swaraj'(No.2),'In Defence of Nationalism' (No.3),'India's Cultural Heritage' (No.45), 'Regeneration of Indian Women' (No.54)

'Women's Education' (No.55),'Communal Unity' (No.59),'The Curse of Untouchability'(No.61),'Religious Tolerance in India' (No.62),'The Problem of Minorities' (No.66).

Parekh,B., Chapter IV ('Satyagraha') and Chapter V ('The Critique of Modernity') in *Gandhi,* OUP, 1997.

Parel ,AJ, (ed), 'Introduction', MK Gandhi, *Hind Swaraj and other Writings,* 1997.

Skinner,Quentin, 'Meaning and Understanding in the History of Ideas', in *Visions of Politics,* Volume I, CUP, Cambridge, 2002.

Recommended Further Readings:

On Theory of Interpretation:

Lyon, David, *Postmodernity,* Viva Books Private Ltd, Delhi, 2002.

Nayar, Pramod K, *Literary Theory Today,*Asia Book Club, New Delhi, 2002 (Chapter-*II)*

Palonen, Kari, *Quentin Skinner: History, Politics, Rhetoric,* Cambridge, Polity Press, 2003.

Powell, Jim, *Postmodernism for Beginners*, Orient Longman, 1998.

————————, *Derrida for Beginners*, Orient Longman, 2000.

Skinner, Quentin, *The Foundations of Modern Political Thought*, Cambridge University Press, 1978.

Tully, James. (ed) *Meaning and Context: Quentin Skinner and his Critics*, Polity Press, UK, 1988.

On Gandhi and his Philosophy:

Ambedkar, BR., *What Congress and Gandhi Have Done to the Untouchables*, Thacker and Co. Ltd., 1945 (For understanding the differences in the approaches towards the removal of untouchability between Gandhi and Ambedkar)

——————————., *Annihilation of Caste*, Blumoon Books, Delhi, 2000.

Andrews, CS., *Mahatma Gandhi's Ideas*, Allen and Unwin, London, 1929.

Bakshi, Rajni., *Bapu Kuti*, Penguin Books India (P) Ltd, New Delhi, 1998 (For an account of how Gandhi's ideas inspired some social workers in India)

Bandopadhya, Anu., *MK Gandhi: Author, Journalist, Printer, Publisher*, Navajivan Publishing House, Ahmedabad,1994(It is a small booklet of mere 20 pages that deals briefly with the aspects of Gandhi mentioned in its title)

Bandopadhyaya, Jayantanuja., *Social and Political Thought of Gandhi*, Allied Publishers, Bombay, 1969.

Bhargava, Motilal, *Role of the Press in the Freedom Movement*, Reliance Publishing House, New Delhi, 1987. p. 384 (Read chapter on Gandhian era)

Bhattacharya, Bhabani, *Gandhi: The Writer*, National Book Trust, New Delhi, 1969(Gives an in-depth account of Gandhi's writing skills and his journalistic endeavours)

----------------., Mahatma *Gandhi,* Arnold Heineman Publishers, New Delhi, 1977.

Bhattacharya, Sabyasachi., *The Mahatma and the Poet,* national Book Trust, India,1999(For the debates between Gandhi and Rabindranath Tagore)

Bondurant, Joan V., *Conquest of Violence: The Gandhian Philosophy of Conflict Resolution,* Princeton University Press, New Jersey 1988.

Bose, Nirmal Kumar, *My Days with Gandhi,* Orient Longman Limited, New Delhi,1974 (For a discussion on the circumstances that led to Gandhi's controversial 'body experiments')

Brock, Peter.,*Gandhi as a Linguistic Nationalist,* South Asia Publications, New Delhi,1996 (For Gandhi's role in the promotion of Indian languages for building a nation)

Brown, Judith, *Gandhi Prisoner of Hope,* Oxford University Press,Delhi, 1992.

Case.,C.M., *Nonviolent Coercion,* George Allen and Unwin.,1923

Chatterjee, Partha *Nationalist Thought in the Colonial World,* London, Zed books, 1986.

Dennis Dalton, *Gandhi's Power :Nonviolence in Action,*(first published by Columbia University Press, 1993) Oxford Indisa Paperbacks, 1998, p. 279 (Read Introduction).

Doke, J.M. *M.K.Gandhi: A Patriot in South Africa,* Publications Division, Government of India, 1994 (This small book gives an insight into Gandhi' s religious beliefs and his influence over his contemporaries)

Erikson Erik H.: *Gandhi's Truth: On The Origins of Militant Nonviolence,* Faber and Faber Limited, London, 1970. p. 97 (For an enquiry into the personal origins of non-violence.

Fischer, Louis, *The Life of Mahatma Gandhi,* Jonathan Cape Thirty Bedford Square, London, 1951.

----------.(ed)., *The Essential Gandhi,* Allen and Unwin, 1962.

Galtung, Johan, *The Way is the Goal,* Gujarat Vidyapith, 1992.

Gandhi, Rajmohan, *The Good Boatman,* Viking, New Delhi, 1995.

--------------., *Mohandas,* Penguin/Viking, 2006.

Green, Martin., *Gandhi:Voice of a New Revolution,* Continuum, New York, 1993.

Gregg, Richard B, *The Power of Non-violence,* Navajivan Publishing House.

Ahmedabad, 1938 (This is one of the earliest comments on the power of non-violence employed by Gandhi and its application the world over)

Horsburgh, *Nonviolence and Aggression :A Study of Gandhi's Moral Equivalent to War,* Lutterworth Press, London, 1972.

Hoyland, John, S., *The Cross Moves East: A Study in the Significance of Gandhi's "Satyagraha",* George Allen and Unwin, London, 1931.

Hunt. James D.,*Gandhi in London,*New Delhi , Promilla and Co., 1978.

Iyer, Raghavan .N .*The Moral and Political Writings of Gandhi,* Three Volumes, Oxford University Press, New Delhi, 1987.

Jordans, JTF.,*Gandhi's Religion: A Homespun Shawl,* Macmillan Press Limited, London, 1998.

Kriplani, Krishna, *Gandhi, A Life,* National Book Trust, Delhi, 1993.

Mehta, Ved., *Mahatma Gandhi and his Apostles,* Penguin Books, 1976 (For a critical view of the Gandhians after Gandhi)

Nanda, BR., *Mahatma Gandhi: A Biography,* George Allen and Unwin Limited, London,1958 (A must read for all students of Gandhi).

———————., *Mahatma Gandhi: A Pictorial Biography,* Publications Division, New Delhi, 1972(An affordable, shorter version of Gandhi's biography)

——————————., *Gandhi and his Critics,* Oxford University Press, Delhi, 1985 (Good reading for understanding the criticism of Gandhi and his response to them)

——————————., *Gandhi, Pan-Islamism, Imperialism and Nationalism,* Oxford University Press, Delhi, 1989.

——————————., (ed) *Mahatma Gandhi – 125 Years,* ICCR, Wiley Eastern Ltd., New Age International Publishers, 1995.

Narain, Jai, *Gandhi's View of Political Power,* Deep and Deep Publications, New Delhi, 1987.

———————., *Economic Thought of Mahatma Gandhi,* Sehgal Publishing Service, Delhi, 1991.

Khare, Prem Shankar, *Press and Public Opinion in India* ,Piyush Prakashan , Allahabad , 1964.(read introduction)

Parekh,Bhikhu, *Gandhi,*(Past Masters, General Editor: Keith Thomas)Oxford University Press, 1997.

———————————., *Gandhi's Political Philosophy: A Critical Examination,* Macmillan, New Delhi, 1989.

———————————, *Colonialism, Tradition and Reform: An Analysis of Gandhi's Political Discourse,* Sage Publications, New Delhi, 1999. (This book contains brilliant discussion on untouchability and Gandhi's concept of religion among other things)

Parel., Anthony .J.,(ed.,) *Hind Swaraj and Other Writings* ,Cambridge Texts in Modern Politics ,Cambridge University Press, 1997.

——————————————(ed),*Gandhi, Freedom and Self-Rule,* Vistaar Publications, New Delhi, 2002.

————————————,*Gandhi's Philosophy the Quest for Harmony,* Vistaar Publications, New Delhi, 2007.

Pinto, Vivek, *Gandhi's Vision and Values: The Moral Quest For Change in Indian Agriculture,* Sage Publications, New Delhi, 1998.

Pyarelal, *The Epic Fast,* Mohanlal Maganlal Bhatt,Ahmedabad, 1932 (This is a daily diary of Gandhi's fast against the Ramsay McDonald Award of 1932)

Radhakrishnan, N., *The Sparks of Nonviolence,* Gandhi Smriti and Darshan Samiti, New Delhi,1998 (It is a unique first person account of the non-violent movements in India and abroad)

Radhakrishnan, S.,(ed) *Mahatma Gandhi: 100 Years,* Gandhi Peace Foundation, New Delhi, 1968 (Contains some of the best tributes to Gandhi from all over the world)

Rolland, Romain ., *Mahatma Gandhi, the Man Who Became One With the Universal Being,* (Translated from French by Catherine D. Groth), Publications Division, Government of India, New Delhi, 1998 (this book was written when Gandhi was still alive. It reflects the respect and awe for Gandhi amongst his contemporaries)

Rudolph, Susanne Hoeber and Rudolph, Llyod I., *Gandhi, the Traditional Roots of Charisma,* Orient Longman India, 1987

– – – – – –, *Postmodern Gandhi, and other essays,* Oxford University Press, New Delhi, 2006.

Sahmat (compiled), *GandhiReconsidered,* Sahmat, Delhi, 2004.

Sarkar, R.C.S., *The Press in India,* Sultan Chand and Company Limited, New Delhi, 1984.

Sharp, Gene., *Gandhi as a Political Strategist: with essays on Ethics and Politics,* Porter Sargeant Publisher, Boston, USA (Introduction by Coretta Scott King; and Sharp's stand that Gandhi was basically a strategist and that nonviolence resistance as a method can be adopted even without its moral content)

Sheean, Vincent, *Mahatma Gandhi, A Great Life in Brief,*

Publications Division, Government of India, New Delhi, 1954.

Shridharani, Krishnalal, *War Without Violence,* Bharatiya Vidya Bhawan, Bombay, 1962.

Verma.M.M .,*Gandhi's Technique of Mass Mobilization.*,R.K. Gupta and Co., New Delhi. 1998. (It is an inquiry into the nature and methods of Gandhi's leadership).

Walker, Roy, *Sword of Gold,* New Delhi., Orient Longman, 1969.

Weber, Thomas *Conflict Resolution and Gandhian Ethics,* Gandhi Peace Foundation, New Delhi, 1991.

----------, *Gandhi's Peace-keeping Army: The Shanti-Sena and Unarmed Peace Keeping Army,* Syracuse, New York, 1996.

Zakaria, Rafiq, *Gandhi and the Breakup of India,* Bharatiya Vidya Bhawan, Mumbai, 1991.

Index